D1274055

busy moms on the GO!

A Busy Mom's Guide to Make-Ahead Meals

suzie roberts

busy moms on the GO!

A Busy Mom's Guide to Make-Ahead Meals

suzie roberts

FRONT TABLE BOOKS
SPRINGVILLE, UTAH

© 2013 Suzie Roberts

All rights reserved.

No part of this book may be reproduced in any form whatsoever, whether by graphic, visual, electronic, film, microfilm, tape recording, or any other means, without prior written permission of the publisher, except in the case of brief passages embodied in critical reviews and articles.

ISBN 13: 978-1-4621-1091-9

Published by Front Table Books, an imprint of Cedar Fort, Inc., 2373 W. 700 S., Springville, UT, 84663
Distributed by Cedar Fort, Inc., www.cedarfort.com

The Library of Congress has catalogued an earlier edition as follows:

Roberts, Suzie.
  Girlfriends on the go : a busy mom's guide to make-ahead meals / Suzie Roberts.
    p. cm.
  ISBN 978-1-59955-015-2
  1. Make-ahead cookery. 2. Cookery (Frozen foods) I. Title.

TX652.R6357 2007
641.5'55--dc22

2007000589

Cover and page design by Erica Dixon
Cover design © 2013 by Lyle Mortimer
Edited by Casey J. Winters

Printed in China

10 9 8 7 6 5 4 3 2 1

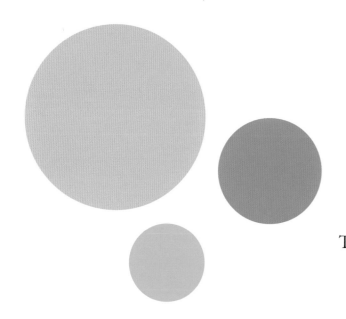

"What's for dinner?" So you say
It's been another crazy day.
Soccer, piano, homework, and more,
I didn't have time to go to the store.
"Let's order out!" The kids say with a grin.
"Pizza again?" says Dad with a cringe.
Then what should we have? Something homemade for sure.
None of this stuff in a box from the store!

"Never you fear," I say with a sigh,
The freezer is full of meals to the sky.
How 'bout lasagna or chicken sweet n' sour?
"Hurry quick, put it in, I have book club in an hour!"
Now there's one more problem left to be solved;
Whose turn to clean up after everyone involved?
"We'll clear our dishes," the kids say and dash.
Mom grabs her book and is out with a flash.
Dad looks around—all these empty seats,
A familiar sight after everyone eats.
It's time for the game; Dad's a huge football fan
But not 'till he throws out the disposable pan.

Contents

Comments from Group Members

"THE MAKE-AHEAD MEAL Group has been such a great thing for my family. I own a childcare center with over 200 children, and I am currently PTA president for an elementary school. With my life being so full, I want to spend every minute with my children as possible. Being part of a casserole club has helped me with that. Dinner isn't stressful, and we can enjoy a home-cooked meal. I think that without the Make-Ahead Meal Group, many of our meals would be fast food, which isn't healthy or cheap."

Ty Singleton, PTA President, business owner

"THE MAKE-AHEAD MEAL Group has simplified my life and has also saved it at times! I always know that there will be a hot meal on the table for my family. I struggle with being creative and trying new things for dinner, but this group has solved both of these problems. We love it and can't imagine life without the group!"

Marci Satterthwaite, PTA President, City Council member

Acknowledgments

I EXPRESS MY gratitude to an awesome friend, Kristen Taylor, for her advice and for letting me "pick her brain" where mine left off. I appreciate her time and talent in editing this book.

THIS COOKBOOK WOULD also not have happened without the help of a great author and friend, Josi Kilpack. Thank you, Josi, for your suggestions and editing.

I EXTEND A sincere thanks to another fabulous friend, Nancy Moyle, for her editing expertise and encouragement.

THANK YOU, DAVE, for being my food critic, for believing in me and encouraging me, and for being the wonderful husband and father that you are. I love you!

TO MY CHILDREN, Kyra, Kuen, Tatem, Bryson, and Mylee: If it weren't for you, there would be no need for me to use my talents and ideas in trying to make our crazy life run smoothly. Thanks for your fun personalities! I love you!

THANKS TO ALL MY "Casserole Club" members, past and present, who have been willing to share their talents with other families. Thanks for going through all the experimental stages of the Make-Ahead Meal Group in order to make this book possible.

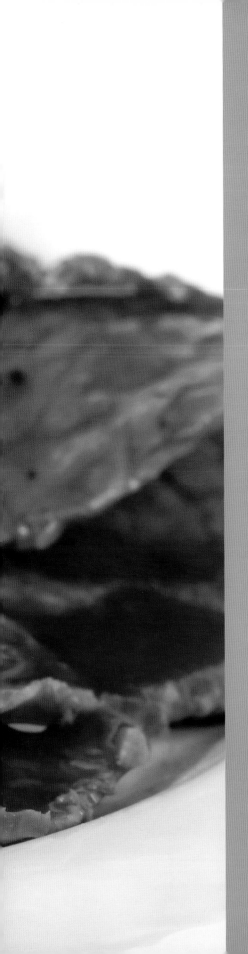

All About Make-Ahead Meals

Introduction

IT'S ONE of those days. You know—*those* days. The phone is ringing off the hook, the kids need help with their homework, your husband is working late, you have a PTA meeting in an hour and still have to pick kids up from soccer practice. Then you think about dinner. Dinner? Okay, here are the quick and easy choices: pizza, pizza, or pizza. Okay, kids . . . how about pizza?

AS YOU fall into bed later that night and analyze your day, you realize that all was running smoothly, one challenge at a time, until 5 p.m. Dinnertime came and you weren't prepared, so everything else seemed to fall apart. Does it seem to be this way more often than not? Do you want it to be different?

THIS BOOK is tailored to the mom who does it all—the mom with a busy life and busy children but who wants to have peaceful, fulfilling family time every night at the dinner table; the mom who wants to feed her family home-cooked meals but wants less time planning and preparing those meals.

WHETHER YOU want to start a Make-Ahead Meal Group or participate in one or just prepare Make-Ahead Meals for your own family, this book is the tool to help you achieve that goal. It will assist you in planning and preparing Make-Ahead Meals that have been tried and tested by actual Make-Ahead Meal Groups. We've picked only the best meals for you and your family.

GOOD LUCK in your endeavors to simplify life, save time and money, enjoy more family time, make some great friends, and be treated to a variety of delicious home-cooked meals.

WHAT IS A MAKE-AHEAD MEAL GROUP?

A MAKE-AHEAD MEAL GROUP is a group of people who prepare and freeze a designated number of the same meal of their choice in the convenience of their own home. Then they get together to exchange dishes so that each member of the group takes home that same number of various meals. It is designed to save time, money, and stress by spending one afternoon making one meal in bulk rather than spending the time every night to prepare a home-cooked meal for your family. This book will give you the tricks of the trade along with many tried and true recipes to help you simplify dinnertime in your own home.

Suzie Roberts

How to Start Your Own Make-Ahead Meal Group

INVITE PEOPLE TO JOIN YOUR GROUP:

THINK OF ALL the moms you know who could use a little simplifying in their lives—maybe your neighbor, friend, sister-in-law, or fellow soccer mom. Think of those moms who are dependable, good cooks, and have healthy homes (clean kitchen habits). These are the types of people you should look for so that you feel good about where your meals are coming from. You may also suggest that your members get a food handler's permit. It isn't necessary, but it's a good idea for food safety. (Call your local health department for information.)

MAKE SOME RULES AND GUIDELINES:

IT IS VERY important that everyone in your group knows exactly what is expected of them so that everyone can do their part. (See page 6 for sample guidelines.) You'll want to have a meeting before your group starts so that everyone can discuss and decide what works best for your specific group. The issues to address are:

- ❁ HOW MANY PEOPLE each meal must feed. For example, many groups set the amount at 6 adult servings, and if the meal is in a casserole dish, require that the dish be 9 × 13 inches in size. For those families that don't eat quite that much, it is perfect for leftovers and to send with your husband to work the next day.

- ❁ DECIDE WHAT PREFERENCES you will cater to. For instance, some groups prefer boneless, skinless chicken breasts. Also, you will need to address food allergies. Many groups find it is easier to not have any food allergy guidelines. However, if the majority of group members prefer low-fat or all-chicken meals, then make it a group requirement.

- ❁ DECIDE A TIME and place to exchange. In case someone can't make it to the exchange on the specified day, it is helpful to make the exchange at a member's house that has extra freezer space. Then those who can't make it to the exchange can deliver their meals the day before and have somewhere to keep it frozen until the other members pick up the meals. Coolers with ice also work well if any group members will be picking up the meals shortly after the exchange.

DECIDE WHEN, WHERE, and how often to exchange meals. Choosing a specific day of each month will help your members always know when it is coming, and they can plan around it. Exchanges can be twice a month or however often your group wants it to be. Choosing a date such as the second Friday of every month is often easier than, for example, choosing the 10th of each month, so that you avoid hitting the weekends.

SET AN APPROXIMATE price range. Otherwise, someone may spend $30 on their meals and someone else may spend $150. A good average is $75. It is feasible to spend less, especially if you watch the sales, but encourage your members not to go over the budget and to choose meals within the budget.

HAVE GROUP MEMBERS bring copies of their recipes to each exchange. A full sheet of paper can be kept in a binder specifically for Make-Ahead Meal recipes. Or exchange 3 × 5 recipe cards to fit in your recipe file. Do whatever works best for group members. Each member should put her name and phone number on her recipe in case other members have questions about it. Side dish suggestions are a helpful addition to each recipe.

DECIDE WHO IS in charge. Your group may want to take turns making reminder calls. Some groups may not even need reminder calls, but it is often appreciated. Most groups choose one person as the president, so to say, and she does all the reminding and finds people to fill vacant spots. This could change every year if desired.

AFTER THE MEETING, send group members a welcome letter or email that includes all the guidelines decided by the group. Make sure each member receives one. This is especially nice for new members who join later. See a sample guideline letter on the next page.

Welcome to the Make-Ahead Meal Group!

HERE ARE THE GUIDELINES:

❀ YOU WILL BE required to make and freeze 10 meals to exchange with our group.

❀ TRY TO SPEND around or below $75 for all costs.

❀ YOUR MEAL SHOULD feed 6 adults. (If item is in a pan, please use a 9 × 13.)

❀ YOU WILL NEED to package your meal either in freezer bags or disposable aluminum pans.

❀ WRITE ON YOUR packaging with permanent marker what the meal is, the basic instructions, and the date (example: Chicken Casserole, 350° for 30 min., 03/01/13). You will probably have to pull the meal out of the freezer ahead of time so that it can thaw. Write the cook time that should be used once the meal is thawed.

❀ PLEASE ONLY MAKE meals that you and your family have tried and enjoy. Don't experiment on the group!

❀ IF YOU ARE stumped about what to cook and what freezes well, there is a great book that has all the tips and recipes that you'll need. It is called *Busy Moms on the Go* by Suzie Roberts.

❀ TYPE UP EACH of your recipes on a full sheet of paper as well as suggestions for what vegetables or side dishes to serve with the meal. We want to be able to put each recipe in its own sheet protector so that we can put together a binder specifically for Make-Ahead Meal recipes. Also, write your name on the recipe page so that we remember who made the meal.

❀ WE WANT EVERYONE to have fun. Obviously your family is not going to love every meal, but hopefully they will enjoy the majority, and that will make it all worthwhile. The most important thing is to take some stress out of your day so that you can spend more time with your family doing fun things, not cooking and cleaning!

❀ ALSO, PAY ATTENTION to your grocery and dining-out budget so that you can see the money you've saved.

Please call if you have any questions!

OUR NEXT MEAL exchange will be on _____ at _____'s house at
_____.

HER ADDRESS IS _____.

PLEASE BRING YOUR meals already frozen. Plan ahead! If you cannot make it to the exchange, please drop off the meals in a cooler (with ice) prior to the exchange. If you are not prepared, each person will keep their meal until you deliver your meal and pick up theirs from each group member. We will meet every second Friday to exchange and tell about our dish. It shouldn't take more than 45 minutes.

FREQUENTLY ASKED QUESTIONS ABOUT MAKE-AHEAD MEAL GROUPS

HOW LONG DOES IT TAKE TO PREPARE 10 MEALS?

❁ IT DEPENDS ON the meal. It usually takes 2–4 hours. We have found that it works best in shifts. For instance, one day you can cook all the meat and the next day assemble the rest. It may sound like a long time, but those ten days that you don't have to take the time and have the mess of preparing meals makes it worth it. With good planning you can save time and frustration by preparing your meals when your kids are asleep or at school.

HOW DOES A MAKE-AHEAD MEAL GROUP SAVE YOU MONEY?

LET ME COUNT the ways . . .

❁ FIRST, YOU GO to the grocery store less often. Do you ever go to the store for milk and bread

and end up coming out with 10 other items you didn't need? The less often you visit the store, the less money you will spend.

❁ YOUR SHOPPING LIST for Make-Ahead Meals is simple. You don't need a list of items for 10 different meals. Instead, you buy 10 of the same thing. Simple is good.

❁ YOU CAN PLAN your meals around what's on sale. If ground beef is on sale, choose a recipe for that month that calls for ground beef.

❁ YOU'LL EAT OUT less. Fridays and Saturdays are great times for Make-Ahead Meals because those are usually the days that you don't feel like cooking. Know your family and pull a meal out of the freezer on days you know you won't have time to cook.

❁ YOU HAVE LESS waste. Since you don't purchase ingredients for several different meals, perishable ingredients don't go bad before you have a chance to use them.

❁ YOU CAN PURCHASE items in bulk. Watch those sales or shop at a warehouse store (like Costco). It's cheaper and leaves less packaging to throw away.

HOW DOES A MAKE-AHEAD MEAL GROUP SAVE YOU TIME?

❁ IF YOU SPEND 4 hours making 10 meals, including prep and cleanup, you will save yourself as much as 16 hours a month. How? If you were to make a meal every night for 10 nights, you would take approximately 15 minutes to decide what you'll have, 30 minutes to run to the store to get the ingredients your missing, and

45 minutes to chop, boil, brown, marinate, simmer, and assemble. Then there are all the dishes, pots, bowls, cutting boards, utensils, and appliances that you used in the preparation process that you need to wash, dry, and put away. That takes you at least another 20 minutes. As you are doing all of this, of course there are at least 15 minutes of interruptions. You don't always realize that it takes so much time to prepare a meal every night, but you will realize the extra time on those 10 nights that you don't have to.

HOW MANY PEOPLE SHOULD BE IN THE GROUP?

✿ EACH GROUP CAN decide for themselves how many meals to make. Most groups find that 10 meals is usually a good amount to exchange each month. That way, you can still fix your family favorites on some days and have leftovers other days. I personally have found that the best use of the meals is to eat them on your busiest days. Maybe Tuesdays are T-ball games and piano lessons. Use a Make-Ahead Meal on those days. I almost always use Make-Ahead Meals on Fridays since that is the day I have found that I don't feel like cooking and would usually order pizza. For many people, Sundays are good for Make-Ahead Meals because it takes less effort to put a nice Sunday dinner on the table—and much less cleanup.

WHAT IF WE HAVE PICKY EATERS?

✿ OBVIOUSLY THERE ARE going to be some meals that members of your family just don't like. Before I started the Make-Ahead Meal Group, I could count on one hand the things

my six-year-old son would eat. However, I felt it was important for him to learn to try new things and believed that if he would try new things, he would like them. Since we always had a variety of food and didn't always have the same old meals that I knew all my kids would eat, he had to learn to try many new things. A year later, he would eat any kind of chicken and some casseroles. For me, that has been the biggest reward from the Make-Ahead Meal Group. Since then, I have had a one-year-old who loves any food I put in front of him. I believe that this acceptance of foods is from having a variety of meals from a young age.

WHAT ARE OTHER BENEFITS OF A MAKE-AHEAD MEAL GROUP?

✿ SOMEONE ELSE'S COOKING: Sometimes food just tastes better when someone else prepares it—not because you're not a good cook, but because you don't have to cook it.

✿ VARIETY: YOU DON'T always have the same old meals. Of course, your family has their favorites, and the days you don't use a Make-Ahead Meal are perfect for those family favorites. People often find meals they'd never considered making have become a new favorite.

✿ SICK DAYS: MOM doesn't get a day off when she's sick—it's nice to have one less thing to do on those days.

✿ DAD'S TURN TO cook: Dad will love the Make-Ahead Meals on those nights he's in charge. With the instructions written right on the package, he can just put a meal in the oven when it's his turn to cook.

✿ SERVING OTHERS: WHEN a friend or a loved

one is having a hard time, it's nice to have a meal that you can easily share. Some people in our Make-Ahead Meal Group choose to make an extra meal each month, and we get together and take the extra meals to someone in need that month, such as a family whose mom or dad is on military duty, a mom who just had a baby, someone having financial troubles, someone who has had a death in the family or a serious illness, and so forth. It's funny how a few meals can take a large burden off someone in need.

WHAT IS THE BEST WAY TO THAW OUR MAKE-AHEAD MEALS?

FOR BEST RESULTS, let frozen meals thaw in the refrigerator for 24 hours. For those of us who don't think that far in advance, here are some other tips:

❖ IF COOKING DIRECTLY from frozen, as a rule of thumb, bump up the temperature 50° higher than the recipe states, and double the time. Generally, this is ample time to cook your frozen meal. You will need to check it periodically to make sure you are on target.

❖ IF YOU WILL be out of the house all day, a slow cooker meal is perfect. You can put it in your slow cooker in the morning and it will be ready at dinnertime. If there are no slow cooker meals in your freezer, your time-delay cook on your oven is also a wonderful tool. Place your meal in the oven at your convenience. Set your bake time about 1½ times the amount called for in the recipe, and set your temperature 25°–50° higher. Your meal will have time to partially thaw in the oven until it starts to cook at the designated time. What a good feeling to walk in to the scent of a nice home-cooked meal after a hard day's work.

WHAT IF SOMEONE QUITS?

IF SOMEONE QUITS, try to fill the spot at as soon as possible. If you are not able to fill that spot in time for the next exchange, you have several options:

1. On the exchange day, tell everyone in your group to take their extra meal home with them.

2. Have everyone exchange their extra meal among themselves so that they take two of another meal home instead of two of their own.

3. Give the extra meals to someone who needs it that month, such as someone who just had surgery or a baby or someone whose spouse is on military duty.

4. Another option is to have a substitute that is willing to participate when someone is unable to do it.

5. Have someone in the group make an extra set of meals and receive double meals that month.

6. If it is early enough, you could call your group and tell them to make one less meal that month. But keep in mind that some members may have already prepared their meals.

• •

FLASH FREEZING

Sometimes you will need to flash freeze items such as meatballs or chicken pockets—anything you will put in a freezer bag in which you don't want individual items to stick together.

To flash freeze, place the items on a cookie sheet and put it in the freezer. As soon as they are no longer soft to the touch, they are ready to be placed in a bag and returned to the freezer.

• •

Make-Ahead Meal Tips

As you are trying to make your life simpler, read all the tips I've learned through years of experience with Make-Ahead Meals. This will save you from having to experiment yourself. I have made it as simple as possible to make it less time consuming and more productive for you. Remember, the people who need Make-Ahead Meals are the ones who don't have time for the small details, just the cold, hard . . . meal!

WHAT TO FREEZE YOUR MEALS IN:

Freezer Bags:

❧ IF AT ALL possible, freeze your meals in freezer bags. They are the cheapest way to go. Many soups, sauces, and non-layered-type casseroles can be frozen in a gallon-size freezer bag.

❧ SQUEEZE AS MUCH air out of the bag as you can. The less air, the less freezer taste and freezer burn your meal will have.

❧ LABEL THE FREEZER bag *before* you freeze it.

❧ ONCE FILLED, LAY your bag flat in the freezer. It will freeze quicker that way and take up less room in the freezer. Don't stack meals on top of each other until after they are frozen so that they can freeze properly in the middle.

Disposable Pans:

❧ DISPOSABLE ALUMINUM PANS work great for anything that can't be put in a freezer bag.

❧ MAKE SURE YOU cover the dish tightly with foil. You may also wish to use a double layer of foil or freezer foil to protect your meals even more. If the meal is tomato based, cover with plastic wrap and then foil. The acid from the tomatoes can eat away the foil.

❧ YOU CAN PURCHASE disposable aluminum pans in bulk at wholesale stores. They end up being about 25 cents apiece. It is so nice to just throw away the mess instead of soaking and scrubbing a pan.

COOKING MEAT IN BULK

WHEN YOU ARE preparing meals for a group, it is easier to cook your meat in bulk. Here are some ways to simplify this process.

❀ GROUND BEEF: CRUMBLE 3 to 4 lbs. on a large cookie sheet with sides. Place in a preheated oven at 425° and bake for 20 minutes or until meat is no longer pink. Make sure you use extra lean or extra-extra lean for this process unless you use a casserole dish with taller sides. Otherwise the grease may drip over the edge. Pull out of the oven when done. Place meat in a colander under hot water. Rinse off extra grease as you use a spatula to crumble the meat.

❀ ANOTHER WAY TO cook ground beef in bulk is to place in boiling water in a stockpot and boil until no longer pink. Then, rinse in a colander as well.

❀ CHICKEN: A LARGE slow cooker will do 10–12 chicken breasts at a time. Place them in the slow cooker with 1 cup of water and cook on medium or high for 2–3 hours (longer if you want to shred it—shorter if you want it whole or to cube it). You can also cook it on low overnight in a slow cooker. Anything you can do while you sleep is a great way to multi-task! Such a motherly thing to do!

❀ ROASTS: USE A large slow cooker for 1–2 roasts, or even better, use a roaster oven to do 5–6 at a time. Cook on medium overnight. When you wake up, they are ready to shred.

FOODS THAT MAY NOT FREEZE WELL

❀ IF YOU ARE making a meal that uses flour tortillas, such as enchiladas, freeze the enchiladas separate from the sauce. Put the sauce in a quart-size freezer bag and freeze along with the meal. Otherwise, your tortillas may get very mushy.

❀ IF YOUR MEAL calls for cooked rice or pasta, undercook it, or it will get mushy from freezing and thawing.

❀ RAW POTATOES or squashes do not freeze well. If you are using potatoes or vegetables that need to be cooked before freezing, undercook them so they don't get mushy. Potatoes tend to get mushy anyway. If possible, replace potatoes with frozen hash browns, which have been commercially prepared for freezing.

❀ SAUCES WITH sour cream, cream cheese, and cream freeze fine. Depending on the ratio of cream in the sauce, you may need to whisk sauce after re-heating since it may separate slightly after freezing.

The Process

Yes, there can be some method to the madness.
....

1. AFTER YOU decide on the meal you want to prepare, check your pantry. Most of the main ingredients called for will probably need to be purchased, but you may already have the spices or other small ingredients. However, don't assume you have enough. You may think you definitely have garlic powder, but if your recipe calls for 1 teaspoon, you will need 10 teaspoons. Nothing is worse than being up to your elbows assembling 10 meals and realizing that you're short one ingredient.

2. AFTER SHOPPING and making sure you have all the ingredients, decide on the pre-meal details. Is it a meal in which the meat needs to be browned, cooked, shredded, or cubed? See our section on cooking meat in bulk for tips on streamlining that process.

3. WHEN YOU'RE getting ready to prepare the meals, get everything out and set in sections around your kitchen, placing each ingredient in order as it is used in the recipe.

❀ OPEN ALL THE items in cans or packages before you start. It saves time and mess. Also, have packaging labeled and ready to fill so that once finished assembling you can place the prepared meal directly into the freezer.

4. YOU CAN choose one of two ways to assemble. If the meal has to be mixed in a bowl, it is easier to mix each meal separately, and then place in the appropriate freezing container.

❀ FOR INSTANCE, IF you are making a soup, go down the line and place all the ingredients in the bowl, mix up, and pour into a freezer bag. If it is a soup that has to be cooked first, you could possibly double or triple the batch in a stockpot to save time. If your meal is something such as a layered casserole, you may want to do it assembly style.

❀ PLACE ALL THE pans out on the table. Prepare the first layer for all 10 meals, place in pan, and move on to the second ingredient. This is very quick and easy.

5. DO NOT stack meals on top of each other in the freezer before they are completely frozen. Stacking makes it hard for the center to freeze in a timely manner.

Soup Recipes

Soups freeze well, and nothing tastes better on a chilly evening.

Cheddar Broccoli Soup

This recipe will make enough for two families.

Breadsticks are always nice to dip in a creamy soup.

1 (16-oz.) pkg. frozen broccoli

6 carrots, sliced

4 stalks of celery, sliced

1 medium onion, chopped

3 cubes butter or margarine

1½ cups flour

10 cups water

10–12 chicken bouillon cubes (to taste)

1 (16-oz.) container Cheez Whiz or Velveeta cheese

❀ STEAM VEGETABLES until almost tender. In a separate bowl, microwave butter or margarine until melted. Stir in flour and mix until smooth. In a large saucepan, dissolve bouillon cubes in boiling water. Add a cup of bouillon water to the butter and flour and whisk together. Then add to boiling water and stir. Add drained vegetables to soup. Add Cheez Whiz or Velveeta cheese. Stir until melted. If freezing, see directions below. Otherwise, serve when hot.

SHOPPING LIST FOR 5 MEALS

5 pkgs. frozen broccoli (abt. 80 oz.)

30 carrots

20 celery stalks

5 medium onions

5 cubes butter or margarine

7½ cups flour

50–60 chicken bouillon cubes

5 (16-oz.) containers Cheez Whiz or Velveeta cheese

FREEZING DIRECTIONS: Cool, then put in a freezer bag. Lay flat in freezer.

Chili

2 lbs. ground beef, browned and
  drained

2 quarts stewed tomatoes

1 pint salsa

30 oz. chili beans, drained

15 oz. kidney beans, drained

15 oz. pinto beans, drained

1 red bell pepper, chopped

1 green bell pepper, chopped

1 onion, chopped

4 Tbsp. brown sugar

salt to taste

cheddar cheese

This recipe will make enough for
two families.

Easy and satisfying—serve with
cornbread and a green salad.

 MIX ALL ingredients together. If freezing, see sidebar. Otherwise, cook in large slow cooker 3–6 hours. To serve, top with shredded cheese.

SHOPPING LIST FOR 5 MEALS

10 lbs. ground beef

10 quarts stewed tomatoes

5 pints salsa

5 large cans chili beans

5 (15-oz.) cans kidney beans

5 (15-oz.) cans pinto beans

5 red bell peppers

5 green bell peppers

5 onions

1¼ cups brown sugar

5 lbs. cheddar cheese

FREEZING DIRECTIONS:

Divide in half. Pour into
gallon-size freezer bags.
Include some shredded
cheese with this meal.

Mexican Chicken Corn Chowder

This mild, south-of-the-border taste will make your taste buds say "gracias"!

1½ lbs. boneless, skinless chicken breasts

½ cup chopped onion

½ tsp. garlic powder

3 Tbsp. butter

2 chicken bouillon cubes

1 cup hot water

1 tsp. ground cumin

2 cups half-and-half

2 cups shredded Monterey Jack cheese

1 (15-oz.) can creamed corn

1 (4-oz.) can chopped green chilies

¼ tsp. hot sauce (Tabasco)

1 bag tortilla chips

❀ IN LARGE saucepan, brown chicken, onion, garlic, and butter. Dissolve bouillon in hot water and add to chicken. Then add cumin and bring to a boil. Reduce heat, cover, and simmer for 5 minutes. Add remaining ingredients. Cook until cheese melts. If freezing, see sidebar. Otherwise, serve topped with crushed tortilla chips.

FREEZING DIRECTIONS:

Pour into a freezer bag and freeze. Include a bag of tortilla chips with the meal.

SHOPPING LIST FOR 10 MEALS

15 lbs. boneless, skinless chicken breasts

5 large onions

5 tsp. garlic powder

abt. 1 cup butter

20 chicken bouillon cubes

abt. ¼ cup ground cumin

5 quarts half-and-half

5 lbs. shredded Monterey Jack cheese

10 (15-oz) cans creamed corn

10 (4-oz.) cans chopped green chilies

2½ tsp. hot sauce (Tabasco)

10 bags tortilla chips

Minestrone

1 lb. ground beef

¼ tsp. seasoned salt

¼ tsp. onion salt

1 tsp. dried onions

2 (10-oz.) cans minestrone soup

1 (15-oz.) can pork and beans

1 (15-oz.) can black beans

2 soup cans water

Spice up a regular can of minestrone soup and serve with a crusty bread.

✿ BROWN GROUND beef with salts and dried onions in a large saucepan. Drain. Add the rest of the ingredients. If freezing, see directions below. Otherwise, simmer 20–60 minutes.

SHOPPING LIST FOR 10 MEALS

10 lbs. ground beef

2½ tsp. seasoned salt

2½ tsp onion salt

3 Tbsp. + 1 tsp. dried onions

20 cans minestrone soup

10 (15-oz.) cans pork and beans

10 (15-oz.) cans black beans

FREEZING DIRECTIONS: Pour into a gallon-size freezer bag. Seal and freeze.

Pasta Fagioli Soup

Taste familiar? Popular Italian restaurants serve this same soup.

1 lb. ground beef, browned and drained

1 small onion, chopped

1 cup grated carrots

1 cup diced celery

1 (15-oz.) can diced tomatoes

1 (15-oz.) can kidney beans, drained and rinsed

2 (15-oz.) cans beef broth

1 tsp. oregano

½ tsp. pepper

2 tsp. fresh parsley, chopped

½ tsp. hot sauce (Tabasco)

1 jar spaghetti sauce

1 small pkg. shell pasta

❄ PLACE ALL ingredients in a large saucepan. If freezing, see sidebar. Otherwise, simmer until vegetables are tender (30–45 minutes).

SHOPPING LIST FOR 10 MEALS

10 lbs. ground beef

5 large onions

20 large carrots

3 bunches celery

10 (15-oz.) cans diced tomatoes

10 (15-oz.) cans kidney beans

20 (15-oz.) cans beef broth

10 tsp. oregano

5 tsp. pepper

abt. ⅓ cup fresh chopped parsley

5 tsp. hot sauce (Tabasco)

10 jars spaghetti sauce

10 small pkgs. shell pasta

FREEZING DIRECTIONS:

Freeze in gallon-size freezer bags.

Taco Soup

1 lb. ground beef, browned and drained

1 (15-oz.) can stewed tomatoes

1 (10-oz.) can tomato soup

1 (10-oz.) can vegetable soup

1 (15-oz.) can corn, drained

1 (15-oz.) can kidney beans, drained and rinsed

¾ cup salsa

1 cup water

2 Tbsp. taco seasoning

2 Tbsp. chili powder

A classic! Kids love eating tacos in a bowl.

✿ MIX ALL ingredients together. If freezing, see directions below. Otherwise, place in a large saucepan and cook until hot. Or heat in slow cooker on low for 3 hours. To serve, pour over crushed corn chips and top with sour cream and shredded cheese.

SHOPPING LIST FOR 10 MEALS

10 lbs. ground beef

10 (15-oz.) cans stewed tomatoes

10 (10-oz.) cans tomato soup

10 (10-oz.) cans vegetable soup

10 (15-oz.) cans corn

10 (15-oz.) cans kidney beans

abt. 2 quarts salsa

abt. 5 pkgs. taco seasoning

1¼ cups chili powder

10 small bags corn chips

10 small tubs sour cream

5 lbs. cheese

FREEZING DIRECTIONS: Pour into a gallon-size freezer bag and freeze. Include a bag of corn chips, a carton of sour cream, and some shredded cheese with this meal. (Do not freeze sour cream.)

Suzie Roberts

Tortilla Soup

Adjust the heat in this soup by using mild, medium, or hot salsa.

1 (16-oz.) can refried beans

1 (15-oz.) can black beans, rinsed and drained

1 (14-oz.) can chicken broth

¾ cup chunky salsa

1½ cups frozen corn

1½ cups cubed, cooked chicken

½ cup water

2 cups shredded cheddar cheese

tortilla chips

dollop of sour cream

✿ COMBINE ALL ingredients except for the cheese, chips, and sour cream. If freezing, see sidebar. Otherwise, simmer for 30 minutes. Crush some tortilla chips in the bottom of the bowls. Add soup and top with sour cream and cheese.

SHOPPING LIST FOR 10 MEALS

10 (16-oz.) cans refried beans

10 (15-oz.) cans black beans

10 (14-oz.) cans chicken broth

2 quarts salsa

5 (16-oz.) bags frozen corn

abt. 10 lbs. boneless, skinless chicken breasts

abt. 5 lbs. shredded cheddar cheese

5 bags tortilla chips

10 small containers sour cream

FREEZING DIRECTIONS:

Place in a gallon-size freezer bag and freeze. Divide a bag of tortilla chips into 2 bags. Put cheese in a freezer bag and include 1 small container of sour cream with each meal. (Do not freeze sour cream.)

Potato and Bacon Soup

3 cans chicken broth

2 cans cream of chicken soup

1 pkg. frozen cubed hash browns

1 lb. bacon, cooked and crumbled

1 small onion, chopped

½ tsp. pepper

¼ tsp. garlic powder

8 oz. cream cheese (not fat-free)

cheese for garnish

This is an easy version
of this comfort food.

✿ MIX TOGETHER chicken broth and cream of chicken soup. Add hash browns, bacon, onion, pepper, and garlic powder. If freezing, see sidebar. Otherwise, cook in slow cooker on low for 5–6 hours. About 1 hour before serving, add cream cheese and heat until thoroughly melted. Top with cheese.

SHOPPING LIST FOR 5 MEALS

30 cans chicken broth

20 cans cream of chicken soup

10 pkgs. cubed hash browns

10 lbs. bacon

10 small onions

5 tsp. pepper

2½ tsp. garlic powder

10 (8-oz.) bricks cream cheese

FREEZING DIRECTIONS:

Pour into a gallon-size freezer bag. Seal and freeze. Include a package of cream cheese with this meal to be added at the end.

Suzie Roberts 23

Beef Recipes

See pages 11–12 for tips on cooking beef in bulk. Ground beef is a great thing to watch the sales for.

Baked Potato Bar

Looking for something different? These potatoes are fun and delicious. This recipe will make enough for two families.

CHILI:

1 lb. ground beef, browned and drained

1 envelope chili seasoning mix

1 (8-oz.) can tomato sauce

½ cup water

1 can kidney beans, drained

CHEESE & BROCCOLI SAUCE:

1 can cream of chicken soup

1 lb. Velveeta cheese

1–2 cups frozen chopped broccoli

TOPPINGS:

sour cream

bacon bits

green onions

shredded cheese

1–2 cups frozen chopped broccoli

✿ CHILI:

Mix all ingredients. Simmer 15 minutes.

✿ SAUCE:

Heat in a saucepan on medium until melted.

✿ IF FREEZING, see next page. Otherwise, scrub 8–10 potatoes. Wrap in foil and pierce several times with a fork. Bake at 400° for 1 hour. Top potato with chili or cheese sauce and your choice of toppings.

SHOPPING LIST FOR 5 MEALS

5 lbs. ground beef

5 envelopes chili seasoning mix

5 (8-oz.) cans tomato sauce

5 cans kidney beans

5 cans cream of chicken soup

5 lbs. Velveeta cheese

3 (16-oz.) pkgs. frozen chopped broccoli

abt. 30 lbs. potatoes

10 (8-oz.) cartons sour cream

10 small pkgs. bacon bits

3 bunches green onions

abt. 4 lbs. shredded cheddar cheese

FREEZING DIRECTIONS: The chili and cheese sauce recipes are enough for 2 meals. Divide the chili and cheese sauce in half and place in quart-size freezer bags. Include with this meal 8–10 potatoes, a carton of sour cream, bacon bits, green onions, and 1½ cups shredded cheese. (Do not freeze sour cream.)

Beef & Bean Burritos

The spaghetti sauce adds a surprisingly good flavor to these homemade burritos.

1–1½ lbs. ground beef, browned

¼ cup chopped onion

1 garlic clove, minced

½ Tbsp. chili powder

½ Tbsp. cumin

salt and pepper to taste

1 (8-oz.) can tomato sauce

1 (16-oz.) can refried beans

8 large flour tortillas

1 jar spaghetti sauce

1 cup shredded cheese (cheddar or Monterey Jack)

IN A saucepan, mix together browned ground beef, onion, and garlic. Add chili powder, cumin, and other seasonings. Stir in tomato sauce and simmer for 10 minutes. Add refried beans; cook and stir until well blended. Cool completely. Warm tortillas in microwave for 30 seconds to soften. Place ½–¾ cup meat mixture on each tortilla. Fold sides of tortilla in and roll up. If freezing, see sidebar. Otherwise, place seam-side down in a baking dish and cover with spaghetti sauce and cheese. Bake at 350° for 30 minutes or until hot and bubbly.

SHOPPING LIST FOR 10 MEALS

10–15 lbs. ground beef

5 large onions

10 cloves garlic

5 Tbsp. chili powder

5 Tbsp. cumin

10 (8-oz.) cans tomato sauce

5 (30-oz.) cans refried beans

8 pkgs. large tortillas

10 jars spaghetti sauce

3 lbs. shredded cheese

FREEZING DIRECTIONS:

Place in a gallon-size freezer bag and freeze. Divide a bag of tortilla chips into 2 bags. Put cheese in a freezer bag and include 1 small container of sour cream with each meal. (Do not freeze sour cream.)

Beef & Cheese Quesadillas

1 lb. lean ground beef

½ cup chopped onion

¾ cup chunky salsa

2 cups shredded Colby-Jack cheese

10–12 flour tortillas

Tortillas freeze well as long as they are kept separate from the liquids in your recipe.

❀ BROWN GROUND beef with onion. Drain. Mix in salsa and cheese. If freezing, see sidebar. Otherwise, spoon approximately ½ cup of meat mixture on one half of tortilla. Fold tortilla in half to close. Arrange quesadillas on baking sheet. Lightly spray tops of tortillas with cooking spray. Bake at 450° for 8 minutes or until lightly browned.

SHOPPING LIST FOR 10 MEALS

10 lbs. ground beef

5 onions

4 (16-oz.) jars chunky salsa

5 lbs. shredded Colby-Jack cheese

10 pkgs. flour tortillas

FREEZING DIRECTIONS:

Place meat mixture in a freezer bag. Include a package of flour tortillas with this meal.

Beef Stroganoff

The longer you cook this, the more tender the meat becomes.

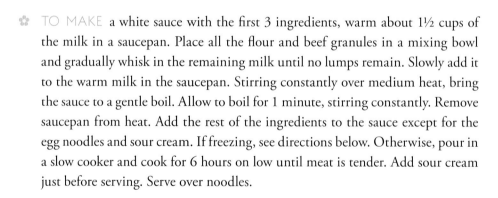

⅓ cup flour

2 cups milk

2 tsp. beef bouillon granules

1–1½ lbs. lean stew meat

½ packet dry onion soup mix

1 bay leaf

1 small can sliced mushrooms

½ cup water

1 small pkg. egg noodles

2 cups sour cream

❁ TO MAKE a white sauce with the first 3 ingredients, warm about 1½ cups of the milk in a saucepan. Place all the flour and beef granules in a mixing bowl and gradually whisk in the remaining milk until no lumps remain. Slowly add it to the warm milk in the saucepan. Stirring constantly over medium heat, bring the sauce to a gentle boil. Allow to boil for 1 minute, stirring constantly. Remove saucepan from heat. Add the rest of the ingredients to the sauce except for the egg noodles and sour cream. If freezing, see directions below. Otherwise, pour in a slow cooker and cook for 6 hours on low until meat is tender. Add sour cream just before serving. Serve over noodles.

SHOPPING LIST FOR 10 MEALS

3⅓ cups flour

20 cups milk

abt. ½ cup beef bouillon granules

10–15 lbs. lean stew meat

5 packets dry onion soup mix

10 bay leaves

10 small cans sliced mushrooms

10 pkgs. egg noodles

10 pints sour cream

FREEZING DIRECTIONS: Cool and place in a freezer bag. Include a pint of sour cream and a package of noodles with each meal. (Do not freeze sour cream.)

Taco Casserole

2 (15-oz.) cans chili

1 can cream of mushroom soup

1 pkg. taco seasoning

2 cups shredded cheddar cheese, divided

1 lb. ground beef, browned and drained

1 pkg. Fritos corn chips

Another simple but fun Mexican-themed dish.

MIX TOGETHER chili, soup, taco seasoning, 1 cup of cheese, and ground beef. If freezing, see sidebar. Otherwise, place the meat mixture in a 9 × 13 pan and top with chips. Bake at 350° for 30 minutes or until bubbly. Take out of oven and top with remaining cheese. Top with other family favorites such as sour cream, olives, tomatoes, and salsa.

SHOPPING LIST FOR 10 MEALS

20 cans chili

10 cans cream of mushroom soup

10 pkgs. taco seasoning

5 lbs. shredded cheddar cheese

10 lbs. ground beef

10 pkgs. Fritos corn chips

FREEZING DIRECTIONS:

Place meat mixture in a gallon-size freezer bag; seal and freeze. Include a bag of Fritos and 1 cup shredded cheese.

Suzie Roberts

Porcupine Meatballs

You would need a porcupine to keep your kids away from these meatballs!

1½ lbs. extra-lean ground beef

½ cup uncooked instant rice

1 tsp. seasoned salt

¼ tsp. salt

½ tsp. pepper

1 Tbsp. dried, chopped onions

2 cans tomato soup

2 Tbsp. Worcestershire sauce

❀ COMBINE GROUND beef, rice, salts, pepper, and onions. Mix well and form into balls. Place in a 9 × 13 pan. Mix together Worcestershire sauce and tomato soup and pour over meatballs. If freezing, see sidebar. Otherwise, cover and bake at 350° for 1–1½ hours until rice is tender. Turn meatballs halfway through baking.

FREEZING DIRECTIONS:

Place in a disposable aluminum pan. Cover with foil.

SHOPPING LIST FOR 10 MEALS

15 lbs. extra-lean ground beef

5 cups uncooked instant rice

abt. ¼ cup seasoned salt

2½ tsp. salt

2½ tsp. pepper

⅔ cup dried, chopped onions

20 cans tomato soup

1¼ cups Worcestershire sauce

Creamy Meatballs

2 lbs. ground beef

2 tsp. salt

1 tsp. pepper

½ onion, grated

3 eggs

2 potatoes, grated

4 carrots, grated

¾ cup milk

If you are short on time, you can buy the meatballs, but this is a terrific, hearty meatball recipe.

SAUCE:

2 cans cream of chicken soup

2 cans cream of mushroom soup

1 can evaporated milk

❧ COMBINE MEATBALL ingredients and form into balls. Place on a cookie sheet and bake at 400° for 20 minutes. Mix sauce ingredients; add cooked meatballs. If freezing, see sidebar. Otherwise, place in a 9 × 13 casserole dish and bake at 350° for 30–45 minutes or until bubbly. Serve over rice or noodles.

SHOPPING LIST FOR 10 MEALS

20 lbs. ground beef

¼ cup salt

3 Tbsp. pepper

5 onions

30 eggs

20 potatoes

40 carrots

7½ cups milk

20 cans cream of chicken soup

20 cans cream of mushroom soup

10 cans evaporated milk

10 pkgs. rice or noodles

FREEZING DIRECTIONS:

Pour sauce over cooked meatballs in a freezer bag. You may want to include a package of rice or noodles with this meal.

Suzie Roberts   33

Easy Swedish Meatballs

It doesn't get any easier than these!

1 pkg. country gravy mix

1 cup sour cream

30 pre-cooked frozen meatballs

1 (12-oz.) pkg. egg noodles

❖ PREPARE GRAVY according to package directions. In a large saucepan, mix prepared gravy with sour cream. If freezing, see sidebar. Otherwise, add frozen meatballs. Heat until meatballs are cooked through and the mixture is bubbly. Serve over prepared noodles.

FREEZING DIRECTIONS:

Mix prepared gravy with sour cream. Place meatballs in a freezer bag and pour sauce over the meatballs.

SHOPPING LIST FOR 10 MEALS

10 pkgs. country gravy mix

abt. 7 pkgs. frozen meatballs (abt. 300 meatballs)

5 pints sour cream

10 (12-oz.) pkgs. egg noodles

Meatloaf

2 lbs. ground beef

1 envelope beefy mushroom soup mix

¾ cup saltine crackers

2 eggs

¾ cup water

⅓ cup ketchup

¼ tsp. seasoned salt

⅛ tsp. garlic salt

¼ cup chopped green pepper (optional)

¼ cup chopped onion (optional)

6 strips bacon

To cut down on the fat content, use extra-lean ground beef and turkey bacon.

❀ COMBINE ALL ingredients except the bacon. Place in a large loaf pan or 2 smaller pans. Cover with strips of bacon. If freezing, see directions below. Otherwise, bake at 350° for 1 hour until done. Let stand for 10 minutes before slicing.

SHOPPING LIST FOR 10 MEALS

20 lbs. ground beef

10 envelopes beefy mushroom soup mix

abt. 1½ boxes saltine crackers (6 sleeves)

20 eggs

3⅓ cups ketchup

2½ tsp. seasoned salt

1¼ tsp. garlic salt

3 large green peppers

3 large onions

abt. 5 pkgs. bacon (60 slices)

FREEZING DIRECTIONS: Place it in 2 disposable aluminum loaf pans, or shape it into a large loaf and place it in a 9 × 13 pan. To freeze, wrap loaf in foil or place in a freezer bag to prevent freezer burn.

Suzie Roberts 35

Italian Meatball Subs

The spaghetti sauce seasoning thickens the sauce perfectly and adds the right balance of flavor.

FREEZING DIRECTIONS:

After cooking, allow to cool. Pour into freezer bags. To serve, heat in a large saucepan. Serve on buns with shredded cheese on top. Include a bag of 1½ cups of shredded cheese and a package of buns.

MEATBALLS:

1 lb. lean ground beef

1 cup Italian bread crumbs

½ cup shredded Parmesan cheese

1 Tbsp. fresh minced parsley (or 1 tsp. dried)

1 garlic clove, minced

½ cup milk

1 egg

SAUCE:

2 (15-oz.) cans tomato sauce

1 (29-oz.) can crushed Italian tomatoes

½ cup shredded Parmesan cheese

2 envelopes spaghetti sauce seasoning

TO SERVE:

hogi buns

shredded mozzarella or provolone cheese

❖ COMBINE MEATBALL ingredients in a large bowl. Set aside. In another large bowl, combine the sauce ingredients and stir until well mixed. Pour about ⅓ of the sauce mixture in the bottom of a large slow cooker. Form the meatballs from the meat mixture and put them in a single layer in the sauce in the slow cooker. Add some sauce to cover the tops and sides of the meatballs. Add more meatballs and cover with more sauce. When all the meatballs are in the slow cooker, pour the rest of the sauce on and cover. Cook on low for 8 hours or high for 4 hours.

SHOPPING LIST FOR 10 MEALS

- 10 lbs. ground beef
- 10 cups Italian bread crumbs
- 10 cups shredded Parmesan cheese
- abt. ⅔ cup fresh minced parsley or 3½ Tbsp. dried
- 1 bulb of garlic
- 5 cups milk

- 10 eggs
- 20 (15-oz.) cans tomato sauce
- 10 (29-oz.) can crushed Italian tomatoes
- 20 spaghetti sauce seasoning envelopes
- 10 pkgs. hogi buns
- 4 lbs. shredded mozzarella or provolone cheese

Suzie Roberts

Mini Meatloaves

Meatloaf is so easy to prepare in large quantities!

¾ cup ketchup

2–3 Tbsp. brown sugar

¾ tsp. dry mustard

1 egg, beaten

3 tsp. Worcestershire sauce

2 cups Chex cereal, crushed

2 tsp. onion powder

½ tsp. seasoned salt

½ tsp. garlic powder

¼ tsp. pepper

2 lbs. ground beef

IN A large bowl, combine ketchup, brown sugar, and dry mustard. Set aside ⅓ cup of this mixture for the topping. Add egg, Worcestershire sauce, crushed cereal, onion powder, seasoned salt, garlic powder, and pepper to mixture. Crumble in ground beef and mix all together. Press meat mixture into 12 muffin cups (about ⅓ cup each). If freezing, see sidebar. Otherwise, bake at 375° for 20–25 minutes. Spoon remaining ketchup mixture on top and bake 10 minutes longer or until meat is no longer pink.

FREEZING DIRECTIONS:

Flash freeze meatloaves in muffin tins. Remove from pan and place in a gallon-size freezer bag. Seal and freeze. These can be baked on a baking sheet after they are thawed. Include topping in a quart-size freezer bag.

SHOPPING LIST FOR 10 MEALS

20 lbs. ground beef

7½ cups ketchup

abt. 1½ cups brown sugar

abt. 2½ Tbsp. dry mustard

10 eggs

⅔ cup Worcestershire sauce

20 cups Chex cereal

abt. ½ cup onion powder

5 tsp. seasoned salt

5 tsp. garlic powder

2½ tsp. pepper

Navajo Tacos

12 Rhodes Texas rolls, thawed and risen

vegetable oil for frying

1 envelope taco seasoning

1 lb. ground beef

1 (15-oz.) can pinto beans

2 cups shredded cheddar cheese

2 cups shredded lettuce

2 medium tomatoes, diced

1 medium onion, chopped

1 cup sour cream

1 cup salsa

This is a fun variation of regular tacos!

✿ FLATTEN EACH roll to a 6-inch circle. Fry each side in vegetable oil at 375° until golden brown. Follow directions on taco seasoning package to prepare ground beef. Add pinto beans and heat through. If freezing, see sidebar. Otherwise, place desired amount of ground beef mixture on warm fry bread. Top with desired toppings.

SHOPPING LIST FOR 10 MEALS

5 bags Rhodes Texas rolls (24 rolls per bag)

10 lbs. ground beef

10 (15-oz.) cans pinto beans

10 envelopes taco seasoning

5 lbs. shredded cheddar cheese

abt. 5 heads lettuce (or divided bags of shredded lettuce to save time)

20 medium tomatoes

10 medium onions

10 small containers sour cream

FREEZING DIRECTIONS:

Place frozen rolls in quantities of 8–10 in a freezer bag. Prepare meat as directed; allow to cool and place in a freezer bag. Include a bag of cheese with the freezer items along with the fresh produce and a carton of sour cream to refrigerate and use within a week. (Do not freeze sour cream.) Have group members use their own salsa.

Smothered Steak

This saucy dish is a real treat after a long day's work.

1½ lbs. stew meat (steak)

⅓ cup flour

½ tsp. salt

¼ tsp. pepper

1 small chopped onion

3 (8-oz.) cans tomato sauce

3 Tbsp. soy sauce

1 can French-style green beans

✿ IF FREEZING, see sidebar. Otherwise, put steak, flour, salt, and pepper in a slow cooker. Stir well to coat meat. Add all remaining ingredients. Cover and cook 6–8 hours. Serve over rice, if desired.

FREEZING DIRECTIONS:

Place flour, salt, and pepper in a freezer bag. Place meat in the bag and shake to coat. Mix all remaining ingredients except green beans together and pour over meat. Freeze flat in freezer. Include the can of green beans with the meal. Mix the beans in the slow cooker with the other ingredients to cook. You may want to include a bag of rice with this meal also.

SHOPPING LIST FOR 10 MEALS

15 lbs. stew meat (steak)

3⅓ cups flour

5 tsp. salt

2½ tsp. pepper

10 small onions

30 (8-oz.) cans tomato sauce or 15 (16-oz.) cans

abt. 2 cups soy sauce

10 cans French style green beans

10 small bags rice

Salisbury Steaks

2 lbs. ground beef (for best results, use the leanest ground beef you can find)

½ cup crushed saltine crackers

2 eggs, slightly beaten

¼ cup milk

1 Tbsp. Savory Herb with Garlic soup mix

2 envelopes beef or mushroom gravy mix

Pair these up with rice, a green salad, and rolls, and you have a simple Sunday meal.

✿ COMBINE GROUND beef, cracker crumbs, eggs, milk, and soup mix. Mix thoroughly. Shape into patties (6–8). If freezing, see sidebar. Otherwise, follow desired cooking directions:

✿ SKILLET METHOD: Brown patties in a skillet. Mix gravy according to package directions, pour over patties, and simmer until done.

✿ SLOW COOKER METHOD: Put patties in a slow cooker. Mix gravy according to package directions and pour over patties. Cook on medium for 4–6 hours.

SHOPPING LIST FOR 10 MEALS

20 lbs. ground beef (extra lean)

1 box saltine crackers

20 eggs

2½ cups milk

1 box (3 pkgs.) Savory Herb with Garlic soup mix

20 envelopes beef or mushroom gravy mix

FREEZING DIRECTIONS:

Place wax paper between each patty or flash freeze. Place in a freezer bag. Include 2 packages of gravy mix with each meal.

Shredded Beef French Dip Sandwiches

Serve this with chips and carrot sticks to make your meal finger-friendly.

1 rump roast

2 envelopes au jus mix

1 pkg. rolls (6–8 deli rolls or 12–18 hard rolls)

❀ PLACE RUMP roast in slow cooker and cook on medium for 3–6 hours until it shreds easily. Halfway through cooking, take the roast out, cut off the fat, and drain juices. Place back in slow cooker. Prepare au jus according to package directions and pour over roast. Cook for the remaining amount of time until it shreds. If freezing, see directions below. Otherwise, serve on rolls and dip in au jus.

SHOPPING LIST FOR 10 MEALS

10 rump roasts

20 envelopes au jus mix

10 pkgs. rolls

> FREEZING DIRECTIONS: Place meat and prepared au jus in a freezer bag. Include a bag of rolls with this meal. To prepare this meal in bulk, you can place approximately 5 roasts in a large roaster oven.

Sloppy Joes

1½ lbs. ground beef, browned

1 chopped onion

¼ tsp. garlic powder

1 (12-oz.) jar chili sauce

½ cup brown sugar

2 Tbsp. vinegar

2 Tbsp. prepared mustard

1 (16-oz.) can tomato sauce

1 pkg. hamburger buns

Filling and hearty—we love these with Tater Tots and fruit salad. Yummy, yummy!

MIX ALL ingredients together. Simmer for 15–20 minutes. If freezing, see sidebar. Otherwise, serve on hamburger buns.

SHOPPING LIST FOR 10 MEALS

15 lbs. ground beef

10 onions

2½ tsp. garlic powder

10 (12-oz.) jars chili sauce

5 cups brown sugar

1¼ cup vinegar

1¼ cup prepared mustard

10 (16-oz.) cans tomato sauce

10 pkgs. hamburger buns

10 pkgs. potato chips (optional)

FREEZING DIRECTIONS:

Freeze in a gallon-size freezer bag. Include a package of hamburger buns (freeze in a freezer bag as well). You might want to include a bag of potato chips with this meal.

Stuffed Green Peppers

The meat mixture is also great just in the muffin tins without the green peppers for small ones who may not like the peppers.

1 lb. ground beef, browned and drained

⅓ cup minced onions

½ tsp. salt

½ tsp. pepper

3 (8-oz.) cans tomato sauce

¾ cup water

½ cup uncooked long grain rice

1 tsp. Worcestershire sauce

1 cup shredded cheddar cheese

6 medium green peppers with tops off and seeds cleaned out

❖ MIX ALL ingredients except cheese and green peppers together. Cover and simmer 15–20 minutes until rice is tender. Stir in cheese. Spoon mixture into green peppers. If freezing, see sidebar. Otherwise, place in muffin tins and bake at 350° for 30–35 minutes.

SHOPPING LIST FOR 10 MEALS

10 lbs. ground beef

4 large onions

5 tsp. salt

5 tsp. pepper

30 (8-oz.) cans tomato sauce or 15 (16-oz.) cans

5 cups long grain rice

10 tsp. Worcestershire sauce

2½ lbs. shredded cheddar cheese

60 green peppers

FREEZING DIRECTIONS:

After spooning the meat mixture into the peppers, wrap peppers in foil and place in a freezer bag to freeze. You can also freeze the meat and the peppers separately.

Tamale Pie

FILLING:

1 lb. ground beef, browned

1 (15-oz.) can corn, drained

1 small can sliced olives

1 clove garlic, minced

1 Tbsp. sugar

1 tsp. salt

1 Tbsp. chili powder

1 (15-oz.) can beans (white, kidney, or pinto), drained

1½ cups shredded cheese

2 (8-oz.) cans tomato sauce

CRUST:

1 cup cornmeal

2½ cups cold water

1½ tsp. salt

This not-too-spicy pie goes over well with little ones who have sensitive taste buds.

❈ COMBINE ALL filling ingredients and place in a 9 × 13 baking dish. Combine crust ingredients in a saucepan on medium to high heat. Stir frequently until thick. Add 1 tablespoon butter and stir until melted. Spread crust mixture on top of meat mixture. If freezing, see sidebar. Otherwise, cover and bake at 375° for 40 minutes.

SHOPPING LIST FOR 10 MEALS

10 lbs. ground beef

10 (15-oz.) cans corn

10 small cans sliced olives

2 bulbs garlic

abt. ⅔ cup sugar

abt. ½ cup salt

abt. ⅔ cup chili powder

10 (15-oz.) cans beans

20 (8-oz.) cans tomato sauce

4 lbs. shredded cheese

10 cups cornmeal

½ cup + 2 Tbsp. butter

FREEZING DIRECTIONS:

Place in a disposable aluminum pan. Cover tightly and freeze.

Suzie Roberts

Sweet & Sour Meatballs

This is a welcome change from your typical sweet and sour recipes.

MEATBALLS:

1 lb. ground beef	½ tsp. Worcestershire sauce
½ cup dry bread crumbs	¼ tsp. pepper
¼ cup milk	¼ cup onion, minced
¾ tsp. salt	1 egg

SAUCE:

½ cup brown sugar	½ tsp. nutmeg
2 tsp. dry mustard	1 cup ketchup

❖ MIX ALL meatball ingredients together and form balls. Bake on a cookie sheet at 400° for 20 minutes. Mix sauce ingredients together. If freezing, see directions below. Otherwise, place meatballs in a slow cooker and pour sauce over them. Mix to coat meatballs and cook on low for 2–3 hours.

FREEZING DIRECTIONS: Place meatballs in a freezer bag and pour sauce over them.

SHOPPING LIST FOR 10 MEALS

10 lbs. ground beef

5 cups dry bread crumbs

2½ cups milk

2½ Tbsp. salt

5 tsp. Worcestershire sauce

2½ tsp. pepper

3 large onions

10 eggs

5 cups brown sugar

abt. ¼ cup dry mustard

5 tsp. nutmeg

abt. 4 (24-oz.) bottles ketchup (total of 80 oz.)

Taco Braid

A new twist on taco night!

1 pkg. taco seasoning

1 lb. ground beef, browned and drained

12 Rhodes rolls, thawed

1 (15-oz.) can refried beans

2 cups shredded cheddar cheese

✿ FOLLOW DIRECTIONS on taco seasoning packet to season ground beef. Roll out rolls together into a rectangle about the length of a cookie sheet. Spread refried beans down the center of the dough. Top with meat mixture and then sprinkle with the shredded cheese. Use a pizza cutter to cut strips along each side of the dough (even numbers on each side). Starting at the bottom, take each piece, cross, and twist. Crisscross dough across top of filling. Continue crisscrossing until your dough is all braided. Carefully place on a greased cookie sheet. If freezing, see sidebar. Otherwise, place on a cookie sheet and bake at 350° for 25–30 minutes until bread is golden brown.

FREEZING DIRECTIONS:

Wrap braid with plastic wrap and then aluminum foil. Freeze.

SHOPPING LIST FOR 10 MEALS

10 lbs. ground beef

10 pkgs. taco seasoning

3 large (36-count) pkgs. + 1 small (12-count) pkg. Rhodes rolls

5 (30-oz.) cans refried beans

5 lbs. shredded cheddar cheese

Cheddar Ranch Sliders

1½ lbs. extra-lean ground beef

1 pkg. dry ranch dressing mix

1 cup shredded cheddar cheese

12 dinner rolls

Mini burgers are way more fun to eat!

✿ MIX ALL ingredients except rolls together. Press into a mini-burger press or spread out and cut with a circle cookie cutter or a drinking glass to get about 2½-inch circles. If freezing, see sidebar. Otherwise, grill and serve on dinner rolls with your favorite condiments.

SHOPPING LIST FOR 10 MEALS

15 lbs. extra-lean ground beef

10 pkgs. dry ranch dressing mix

10 cups shredded cheddar cheese

120 dinner rolls

FREEZING DIRECTIONS:

Flash freeze and place in a gallon-size freezer bag. Include a package of dinner rolls with this meal.

Cheesy Macaroni & Beef

Better than the
boxed stuff!

12 oz. elbow macaroni

1 (28-oz.) can whole tomatoes,
   pureed

¼ tsp. salt

⅛ tsp. pepper

2 cloves garlic, minced

1 lb. ground beef, browned with 1
   chopped onion

1 cup grated mozzarella cheese

1 cup grated cheddar cheese

❁ COOK THE elbow macaroni according to the package directions, cutting the time in half. Drain. In a large bowl, mix together the tomatoes, salt, pepper, garlic, and browned ground beef. Add the half-cooked macaroni. If freezing, see sidebar. Otherwise, place in a 9 × 13 baking dish, cover with foil, and bake at 400° for about 45 minutes or until bubbly. Then take out, remove foil, cover with cheeses, and broil until cheese is melted and browned on top.

SHOPPING LIST FOR 10 MEALS

120 oz. elbow macaroni

10 (28-oz.) cans whole tomatoes

2½ tsp. salt

1¼ tsp. pepper

3 bulbs garlic

10 lbs. ground beef

10 small onions

10 cups grated mozzarella cheese

10 cups grated cheddar cheese

FREEZING DIRECTIONS:

Place in a disposable pan and cover with foil. Include the grated cheeses in a bag to be added after baking.

Beef Teriyaki

2 Tbsp. cornstarch

1 (14-oz.) can beef broth

2 Tbsp. soy sauce

1 Tbsp. brown sugar

¼ tsp. garlic powder

2 lbs. boneless beef sirloin, sliced into thin strips (to make slicing easier, freeze meat for 1 hour)

1 (12-oz.) pkg. frozen broccoli florets

rice for garnish

Could it really be this easy?

❀ MIX TOGETHER the cornstarch, beef broth, soy sauce, brown sugar, and garlic powder. Set aside. Stir-fry beef in a skillet until browned. Add liquid to skillet. Cook until mixture boils and thickens, stirring constantly. If freezing, see sidebar. Otherwise, add broccoli and cook until broccoli is heated through. Serve over rice.

SHOPPING LIST FOR 10 MEALS

1¼ cups cornstarch

10 (14-oz.) cans beef broth

1¼ cups soy sauce

⅔ cup brown sugar

2½ tsp. garlic powder

20 lbs. boneless beef sirloin (having the butcher cut in strips will save a lot of time)

10 (12-oz.) packages frozen broccoli florets

FREEZING DIRECTIONS:

Pour in gallon-size freezer bag, seal, and freeze. Include a package of broccoli florets with this meal.

Taco Stuffed Shells

These aren't your traditional pasta shells.

1½ lbs. ground beef, browned

1 envelope taco seasoning

1 (8-oz.) brick cream cheese

18 uncooked jumbo pasta shells

3 Tbsp. butter, melted

1 cup salsa

½ cup taco sauce

1 cup shredded cheddar cheese

❀ COOK BEEF and taco seasoning according to the taco seasoning directions. Add cream cheese. Simmer until melted and mix well. Chill for 1 hour. Cook pasta according to package directions but half the time. Gently toss with butter. Fill each shell with about 3 Tbsp. of the filling. If freezing, see sidebar. Otherwise, pour salsa in the bottom of a 9 × 13 pan. Place shells in pan. Top each one with taco sauce. Cover and bake at 350° for 30 minutes. Uncover, sprinkle with cheese, and bake 10 more minutes or until cheese is melted. Top with desired toppings, such as sour cream, onions, crushed tortilla chips, and tomatoes.

FREEZING DIRECTIONS:

Remember to undercook the pasta shells. Pour salsa in the bottom of a disposable pan. Place shells in pan. Top each one with taco sauce. Cover with foil and freeze.

SHOPPING LIST FOR 10 MEALS

15 lbs. ground beef

10 envelopes taco seasoning

10 (8-oz.) bricks cream cheese

180 jumbo pasta shells

1 lb. butter

10 cups salsa

5 cups taco sauce

10 cups shredded cheddar cheese

Steak Fajitas

1½–2 lbs. sirloin steak, thinly sliced

¼ cup lime juice

¼ cup white wine vinegar

3 Tbsp. olive oil

2 tsp. oregano

1 tsp. cumin

½ tsp. chili powder

3 cloves garlic, minced

1–2 green peppers, cut into thin strips

1 onion, sliced

10 flour tortillas

You could use chicken or a combination of steak and chicken if you'd like!

✿ IF FREEZING, see sidebar. Otherwise, place steak in a skillet. Mix together lime juice, vinegar, olive oil, oregano, cumin, chili powder, and garlic. Pour over steak. Add peppers and onions. Cook over medium heat until steak is cooked through.

SHOPPING LIST FOR 10 MEALS

15–20 lbs. sirloin steak (have the butcher slice to save time)

2½ cups lime juice

2½ cups white wine vinegar

2 cups olive oil

7 Tbsp. oregano

3 Tbsp. + 1 tsp. cumin

5 tsp. chili powder

3 bulbs garlic

10–20 green peppers

10 onions

10 pkgs. flour tortillas

FREEZING DIRECTIONS:
Place steak in a gallon-sized freezer bag. Mix together lime juice, vinegar, olive oil, oregano, cumin, chili powder, and garlic. Pour over steak. Seal and freeze. Freeze the peppers and onions in a separate bag. Include a package of flour tortillas with this meal.

Best Sunday Roast

This is my family's favorite Sunday dinner.

1 rump roast

3 pkgs. beef gravy mix

1 pkg. dry Italian dressing mix

1 pkg. dry ranch dressing mix

3 cups water

✿ IF FREEZING, see sidebar. Otherwise, place roast in a slow cooker. In a small bowl, mix together the remaining ingredients. Pour over roast. Cook on low for 6–8 hours. The roast will fall apart, and the gravy is delicious to have over mashed potatoes!

FREEZING DIRECTIONS:

Place roast in a gallon-sized freezer bag. Pour mixture over and freeze.

SHOPPING LIST FOR 10 MEALS

10 rump roasts

30 pkgs. beef gravy mix

10 pkg. dry Italian dressing mix

10 pkgs. dry ranch dressing mix

Chicken Recipes

See pages 11–12 for ideas on cooking chicken in bulk. If it is a slow cooker meal, freeze in a bag.

Barbecue Chicken Sandwiches

Your favorite barbecue restaurant doesn't even compare to the tangy barbecue sauce in these sandwiches!

1 cup ketchup

1 cup vinegar

½ cup molasses

½ cup honey

1 tsp. liquid smoke

½ tsp. salt

¼ tsp. garlic powder

¼ tsp. onion powder

¼ tsp. hot sauce (Tabasco; optional)

2–3 lbs. boneless, skinless chicken breasts

✿ COMBINE ALL ingredients except chicken in a saucepan over high heat. Blend with a whisk until smooth. When the mixture comes to a boil, add the chicken. Turn the heat down and simmer for 45–60 minutes. Once the chicken is tender enough to shred and the sauce is thickened, remove from heat and shred the chicken with two forks. If freezing, see directions below. Otherwise, serve on buns.

SHOPPING LIST FOR 10 MEALS

30 lbs. boneless skinless chicken breasts

10 cups ketchup

10 cups vinegar

5 cups molasses

5 cups honey

abt. ¼ cup liquid smoke

5 tsp. salt

2½ tsp. garlic powder

2½ tsp. onion powder

2½ tsp. hot sauce (Tabasco)

10 pkgs. buns

FREEZING DIRECTIONS: After shredding the chicken, allow to cool. Pour into a freezer bag. You can also cook this in a slow cooker.

Breaded Ranch Chicken

1 cup Italian-style bread crumbs

3 Tbsp. minced onions

1 lb. cooked bacon, crumbled (or 1 cup pre-cooked bacon pieces)

6 boneless, skinless chicken breasts

1 cup ranch dressing

This chicken will have your mouth watering for more.

❖ MIX BREAD crumbs, onions, and bacon together. Dip chicken in ranch and then cover with bread crumb mixture. If freezing, see sidebar. Otherwise, place in a 9 × 13 pan and bake at 375° for 1 hour.

SHOPPING LIST FOR 10 MEALS

abt. 30 lbs. boneless, skinless chicken breasts

5 (16-oz.) bottles ranch dressing

10 cups Italian style bread crumbs

abt. 2 cups minced onions

10 lbs. bacon (or 10 cups pre-cooked bacon pieces)

FREEZING DIRECTIONS:

Place in a disposable aluminum pan; cover with foil and freeze.

Cheesy Italian Chicken

Easy and cheesy—this is a dish that gets repeat requests!

2 cans cream of chicken soup

¾ cup milk

¾ cup Italian bread crumbs

2 cups Monterey Jack cheese

4–6 boneless, skinless chicken breasts, cut in pieces

✿ IF FREEZING, see sidebar. Otherwise, mix soup, milk, bread crumbs, and cheese together. Add chicken pieces. Cook in slow cooker on low for 6–8 hours. Stir often so cheese doesn't stick to the bottom. Serve over rice or noodles.

SHOPPING LIST FOR 10 MEALS

20 to 30 lbs. boneless, skinless chicken breasts

20 cans cream of chicken soup

abt. 2 quarts milk

7½ cups Italian bread crumbs

5 lbs. shredded Monterey Jack cheese

10 small bags rice

FREEZING DIRECTIONS:

Place chicken pieces in a freezer bag. Mix all other ingredients together and pour over chicken in the bag. You may want to include a bag of rice with this meal.

Chicken Cordon Bleu

6 chicken breasts

⅔ cups Italian bread crumbs

½ cup Parmesan cheese

12 slices deli ham

6 slices provolone cheese

½ cup butter or margarine, melted

❀ POUND CHICKEN breasts until they are ½ inch thick. In a medium-sized bowl, mix bread crumbs and Parmesan cheese. Put 2 slices of ham on the chicken. Roll up a slice of provolone cheese and place in the center of meat. Roll up meat and secure with a toothpick. Dip in melted butter and then in bread crumb mixture. If freezing, see sidebar. Otherwise, place seam-side down on cookie sheet. Cover and bake at 350° for 30 minutes or until chicken is no longer pink.

❀ OPTIONAL: You can also use turkey tenders for this recipe.

SHOPPING LIST FOR 10 MEALS

60 chicken breasts

60 slices provolone cheese

120 slices deli ham

5 cups butter or margarine

abt. 7 cups Italian bread crumbs

5 cups Parmesan cheese

60 toothpicks

FREEZING DIRECTIONS:

Place in a freezer bag and freeze.

Chicken Broccoli Rice Bake

Comfort food at its best!

1 pkg. chicken-flavored rice mix (prepared according to pkg. directions)

2 Tbsp. butter or margarine (to prepare rice)

1 (16-oz.) pkg. frozen broccoli

4 chicken breasts, cooked and cut up

2–3 cups shredded cheddar cheese

1 sleeve crushed saltine crackers

2 Tbsp. butter or margarine

SAUCE

2 cans cream of chicken soup

1 cup mayonnaise

2 tsp. lemon juice

1 Tbsp. curry powder (optional)

¼ cup milk

❖ SPREAD PREPARED rice in the bottom of a 9 × 13 baking dish. Mix sauce ingredients together. Spread ⅓ of the sauce over rice. Layer the broccoli and spread ⅓ of the sauce on top. Evenly spread chicken on top of the sauce and add remaining sauce on top. Top with cheese. If freezing, see directions below. Otherwise, top with crushed crackers and dabs of butter (butter optional). Bake at 375° for 45–55 minutes.

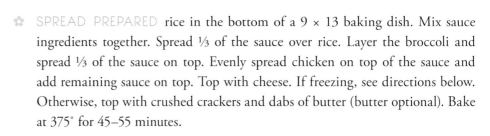

FREEZING DIRECTIONS: Slightly undercook rice to freeze. Place meal in a disposable aluminum pan; cover and freeze. Before baking, top with crushed crackers and dabs of butter (butter optional). Include butter and crackers along with this meal.

SHOPPING LIST FOR 10 MEALS

20 lbs. chicken breasts

10 pkgs. chicken flavored rice mix

10 pkgs. frozen broccoli

6 lbs. shredded cheddar cheese

3 pkgs. saltine crackers (with 4 sleeves each)

2½ cups butter or margarine

20 cans cream of chicken soup

3 (32-oz.) jars mayonnaise

abt. ¼ cup lemon juice

⅔ cup curry powder (optional)

2½ cups milk

Chicken Divan

Leave the curry out if there are sensitive taste buds in your home. However, it does add a nice kick!

2 (10-oz.) pkgs. chopped broccoli

6 boneless skinless chicken breasts, cooked and diced

1 cup mayonnaise

2 cans cream of chicken soup

1 tsp. lemon juice

1 tsp. curry powder

1 cup shredded cheddar cheese

½ cup dry bread crumbs

2 Tbsp. melted butter

❖ COOK BROCCOLI as directed on package. Drain. Mix all ingredients except cheese, bread crumbs, and melted butter. If freezing, see sidebar. Otherwise, place in a 9 × 13 casserole dish. Cover with cheese. Mix the bread crumbs with the melted butter and sprinkle on top. Bake at 350° for 25 minutes. Serve over cooked rice.

SHOPPING LIST FOR 10 MEALS

60 boneless, skinless chicken breasts

20 (10-oz.) pkgs. chopped broccoli

10 cups mayonnaise

20 cans cream of chicken soup

abt. ¼ cup lemon juice

abt. ¼ cup curry powder

10 cups shredded cheddar cheese

5 cups bread crumbs

1¼ cup butter

FREEZING DIRECTIONS:

Slightly undercook broccoli. Place in a disposable aluminum pan and cover tightly with foil. Include cheese and bread crumbs with this meal.

Chicken Macaroni Bake

2 cups chicken, cooked and cubed

1½ cups uncooked elbow macaroni

2 cups shredded cheddar cheese

1 can cream of chicken soup

1 cup milk

1 (8-oz.) can mushrooms (optional), drained

¼ tsp. pepper

Homemade macaroni-and-cheese taste with less work.

❀ IN A large bowl, combine the chicken, macaroni, cheese, soup, milk, mushrooms, and pepper. If freezing, see sidebar. Otherwise, pour into a greased 9 × 13 pan. Cover and bake at 350° for 60–65 minutes or until macaroni is tender.

SHOPPING LIST FOR 10 MEALS

abt. 20 lbs. boneless, skinless chicken breasts

15 cups elbow macaroni

5 lbs. shredded cheddar cheese

10 cans cream of chicken soup

2½ quarts milk

10 (8-oz.) cans mushrooms (optional)

2½ tsp. pepper

FREEZING DIRECTIONS:

May freeze in a freezer bag or a disposable aluminum pan.

Chicken Pockets

To save time, you can use refrigerator crescent rolls, but the homemade dough is well worth the effort.

DOUGH (2-HOUR FRENCH BREAD DOUGH):

1 Tbsp. + 1 tsp. yeast

3 Tbsp. sugar

½ cup warm water

1 Tbsp. salt

⅓ cup oil

2 cups very hot tap water

6 cups flour

CHICKEN POCKETS:

8 oz. cream cheese

4 Tbsp. melted butter

½ tsp. salt

¼ tsp. pepper

2 Tbsp. chopped green onions

2 cups cooked and cubed chicken

4 Tbsp. milk

1 batch 2-hour French bread dough

1½ cups Italian bread crumbs

melted butter (additional)

CHICKEN GRAVY:

1 can cream of chicken soup

¾ cup water or milk

❖ DISSOLVE YEAST and sugar in ½ cup water. In a large bowl, combine salt, oil, and 2 cups hot water. Mix in 3 cups flour. Add the yeast mixture. Mix in remaining 3 cups of flour. Punch down every 10 minutes for 50 minutes. If making Chicken Pockets, continue on to the next part of the recipe. If making French bread, shape, and let rise until double. Bake at 400° for 20 minutes. (Also great for sweet rolls.)

❀ FOR CHICKEN Pockets, blend cream cheese and melted butter until smooth in a large bowl. Add the remaining ingredients except bread dough, bread crumbs, and additional melted butter. Roll out bread dough and cut into 3-inch squares. Place ½ cup of chicken mixture in the center of each square. Pull up the corners and seal the edges. Roll in melted butter and then in bread crumbs. Let rise until double in size. If freezing, see sidebar on previous page. Otherwise, bake at 350° for 20 minutes or until golden brown. Serve with chicken gravy.

❀ FOR GRAVY, empty can of soup into saucepan and whisk in water or milk. Heat until very warm, stirring continually. Serve over Chicken Pockets.

SHOPPING LIST FOR 10 MEALS

abt. 1 cup yeast

abt. 2 cups sugar

¾ cup salt

3⅓ cups oil

60 cups flour

10 pkgs. cream cheese

5 cubes butter

2½ cups milk

2½ tsp. pepper

15 cups Italian bread crumbs

2 bunches green onions

10 cans cream of chicken soup

12 lbs. boneless, skinless chicken breasts

Chicken Marengo

The combination of these ingredients makes a great flavorful chicken.

1 can tomato soup

1 can Golden Mushroom soup

1 can mushrooms, drained

½ cup chopped onion

6 boneless, skinless chicken breasts

✿ MIX SOUPS, mushrooms and onion. If freezing, see sidebar. Otherwise, pour mixture over chicken in slow cooker and cook on low for 6–8 hours. Serve over warm noodles.

FREEZING DIRECTIONS:

Place chicken in freezer bag. Pour mixture over chicken and seal. Include a package of noodles with this meal.

SHOPPING LIST FOR 10 MEALS

60 boneless, skinless chicken breasts (abt. 30 lbs.)

10 cans tomato soup

10 cans Golden Mushroom soup

10 cans mushrooms

5 onions

10 bags egg noodles

Chicken Noodle Casserole

1 (16-oz.) pkg. wide egg noodles

½ cup mayonnaise

½ cup milk

1 can cream of chicken soup

1 large can chicken (drained)

2 cups shredded cheddar cheese
(divided)

garlic salt to taste

seasoned salt to taste

dash of pepper

1 small can French's onions

You can never have too many great chicken recipes.

❁ COOK NOODLES according to package directions. In a large mixing bowl, mix together mayonnaise, milk, soup, and chicken. Season to taste. Drain the pasta; stir into chicken mixture. Then stir in 1 cup of cheese. Add the remaining cup of cheese on top and top with onions. If freezing, see sidebar. Otherwise, bake at 425° for 20–25 minutes until bubbly.

SHOPPING LIST FOR 10 MEALS

10 (16-oz.) pkgs. of noodles

5 cups mayonnaise

5 cups milk

10 cans cream of chicken soup

10 large cans chicken

20 cups shredded cheddar cheese

abt. 3 Tbsp. garlic salt

abt. 3 Tbsp. seasoned salt

abt. 2 Tbsp. pepper

10 small cans French's onions

FREEZING DIRECTIONS:

When preparing, undercook the noodles. Put in a disposable aluminum pan and cover tightly with foil. If you bake this casserole from frozen, keep it covered for the first half of baking.

Chicken Tetrazzini

You can also use leftover turkey in this terrific recipe.

8 oz. spaghetti, broken in pieces

5 Tbsp. butter or margarine

6 Tbsp. flour

3 cups chicken broth

1 cup light cream

1 tsp. salt

dash of pepper

1 small can mushrooms, undrained

5 Tbsp. minced green peppers

3 cups cooked chicken, cubed

½ cup shredded Parmesan cheese

1 cup shredded cheddar cheese

FREEZING DIRECTIONS:

Slightly undercook spaghetti. Place in a disposable aluminum pan; cover and freeze.

❖ COOK SPAGHETTI according to package directions. In a medium saucepan, melt butter and blend in flour. Stir broth into mixture and add cream. Cook until mixture thickens and bubbles, stirring constantly. Add salt, pepper, drained spaghetti, mushrooms, green peppers, and cooked chicken. Place in a 9 × 13 pan and sprinkle with Parmesan and cheddar cheese. If freezing, see sidebar. Otherwise, bake at 350° for 30–45 minutes until bubbly and lightly browned.

SHOPPING LIST FOR 10 MEALS

10 (8-oz.) pkgs. spaghetti

3¼ cups butter or margarine

3¾ cups flour

30 cups chicken broth

5 pints light cream

abt. ¼ cup salt

abt. 2 Tbsp. pepper

10 small cans mushrooms

5 green peppers

15 lbs. boneless skinless chicken breasts

5 cups Parmesan cheese

2½ lbs. shredded cheddar cheese

Company's Coming Chicken

2½ cups chicken, cooked and cubed

2 cups sour cream

1 can cream of mushroom soup

1½ cups Monterey Jack cheese, shredded

½ cup chopped green onions

½ cup chopped celery

1 pkg. stuffing, prepared

Don't save this one for company—it's too good!

✿ PLACE CHICKEN in a 9 × 13 pan. Combine sour cream, soup, cheese, green onions, and celery. Spoon mixture over chicken. Prepare stuffing and sprinkle over mixture. If freezing, see sidebar. Otherwise, bake at 375° for 35–40 minutes.

SHOPPING LIST FOR 10 MEALS

abt. 15 lbs. boneless, skinless chicken breasts

10 pints sour cream

10 cans cream of mushroom soup

4 lbs. shredded Monterey Jack cheese

8 bunches green onions

3 bunches celery

10 pkgs. stuffing

FREEZING DIRECTIONS:

Place in a disposable aluminum pan and cover tightly with foil to freeze..

Suzie Roberts   69

Creamy Bacon Chicken

Rich and creamy!

5–6 boneless, skinless chicken breasts

1 (3-oz.) pkg. precooked bacon bits (not artificial)

1 can roasted garlic cream of mushroom soup

1 can cream of mushroom soup

1 cup sour cream

½ cup flour

❖ IF FREEZING, see sidebar. Otherwise, place chicken in slow cooker. Mix all remaining ingredients together and pour over chicken. Cook on low for 6–8 hours. Serve over egg noodles.

SHOPPING LIST FOR 10 MEALS

abt. 30 lbs. boneless, skinless chicken breasts

10 (3-oz.) pkgs. precooked bacon bits (not artificial)

10 cans roasted garlic cream of mushroom soup

10 cans cream of mushroom soup

5 pints sour cream

5 cups flour

10 pkgs. egg noodles

FREEZING DIRECTIONS:

Place chicken in a gallon-size freezer bag. Pour sauce mixture over chicken. Seal and freeze. You may want to include a bag of egg noodles with this meal.

Divine Crockpot Chicken

5–6 boneless, skinless chicken breasts

1 can cream of celery soup

1 can cream of mushroom soup

1 envelope dry onion soup mix

1 tsp. dried parsley

IF FREEZING, see sidebar. Otherwise, place chicken in slow cooker. Mix all other ingredients together and pour over chicken. Cook on low for 4–6 hours. Serve over pasta or rice.

SHOPPING LIST FOR 10 MEALS

abt. 30 lbs. boneless, skinless chicken breasts

10 cans cream of celery soup

10 cans cream of mushroom soup

5 pkgs. (2 envelopes each) dry onion soup mix

3⅓ Tbsp. dried parsley

10 small bags of rice or egg noodles

Slow cooker meals are perfect for warm summer days because you don't have to heat up your oven.

FREEZING DIRECTIONS:

Place chicken in a gallon-size freezer bag. Pour sauce over chicken. Seal and freeze. You can substitute thin pork chops for the chicken in this recipe. You may want to include a package of rice or egg noodles with this meal.

Easy Chicken Pot Pie

Frozen pie crusts cut your preparation time to almost nothing.

1 can cream of chicken soup

¼ cup milk or cream

1 (16-oz.) bag frozen mixed vegetables or 2 cups various veggies of your choice

3 boneless, skinless chicken breasts, cooked and diced

1 (double) ready-to-bake pie crust

seasonings to taste

❧ MIX TOGETHER soup and milk until smooth. Stir in veggies. Add chicken and mix. Pour into pie crust. Cover with top crust. Cut 3–6 slits in top of crust. If freezing, see directions below. Otherwise, bake at 400° for 30–40 minutes. Top crust should be golden brown. Cool for 15 minutes before serving.

SHOPPING LIST FOR 10 MEALS

abt. 15 lbs. boneless, skinless chicken breasts

10 bags frozen mixed vegetables

10 cans cream of chicken soup

2½ cups milk or cream

10 double pie crusts

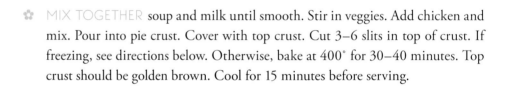

FREEZING DIRECTIONS: Place in a freezer bag or 9 × 13 disposable aluminum pan; cover with foil and freeze.

Easy Cheesy Chicken

6 boneless, skinless chicken breasts

1 can cream of mushroom soup

1 can cream of chicken soup

2 cups sour cream

2 cups cheddar cheese

dash of paprika

Simple, creamy, cheesy—a real crowd pleaser.

❖ PLACE CHICKEN breasts in a greased 9 × 13 pan. Mix all other ingredients and pour over chicken. If freezing, see sidebar. Otherwise, bake uncovered at 350° for 1½–2 hours or until chicken is tender. Serve over rice or egg noodles.

SHOPPING LIST FOR 10 MEALS

abt. 30 lbs. boneless, skinless chicken breasts

10 cans cream of mushroom soup

10 cans cream of chicken soup

10 pints sour cream

5 lbs. shredded cheddar cheese

1 tsp. paprika

10 small bags rice or egg noodles

FREEZING DIRECTIONS:

Place in a disposable aluminum pan and cover with foil. You may want to include a bag of rice or egg noodles with this meal.

Hawaiian Chicken

A sweet way to enjoy your chicken.

6 boneless, skinless chicken breasts

½ cup ketchup

½ tsp. Worcestershire sauce

1 tsp. mustard

½ cup crushed pineapple with juice

½ cup brown sugar

❀ IF FREEZING, see sidebar. Otherwise, put chicken in a 9 × 13 pan. Mix remaining ingredients together and pour over chicken. Bake at 350° for 45 minutes or stew in slow cooker for 4–6 hours. Serve over rice.

SHOPPING LIST FOR 10 MEALS

30 lbs. boneless, skinless chicken breasts

5 cups ketchup

5 tsp. Worcestershire sauce

10 tsp. mustard

2 cans crushed pineapple

5 cups brown sugar

10 bags rice

FREEZING DIRECTIONS:

Place chicken in a freezer bag. Pour sauce mixture over chicken in bag. You may want to include rice with this meal.

Lemon Chicken

6 boneless, skinless chicken breasts

3 tsp. dried thyme

3 tsp. salt

1 clove garlic

1 cup lemon juice

This chicken has quite the zing! Pair it with Dill-Lemon Rice for a flavorful meal.

✿ MIX SPICES and lemon juice in a bag. Add chicken breasts. If freezing, see directions below. Otherwise, marinate for several hours or overnight. Place in slow cooker for 4–6 hours on low. You can also bake or grill instead.

SHOPPING LIST FOR 10 MEALS

abt. 30 lbs. boneless, skinless chicken breasts

abt. ²/₃ cup dried thyme

abt. ²/₃ cup salt

2 bulbs of garlic

10 cups lemon juice (80 oz.)

FREEZING DIRECTIONS: Place in a freezer bag. The chicken will marinate while thawing.

Dill-Lemon Rice

Pair this with Lemon Chicken for a zingy meal.

3 cups long grain rice, uncooked

3 tsp. grated lemon peel

2½ tsp. dill weed

1 tsp. salt

2 Tbsp. instant chicken bouillon powder

❀ COMBINE ALL ingredients in a large bowl and blend well. Store in a cool, dry place and use within 6–8 months.

❀ TO PREPARE: Combine Dill-Lemon Rice mix, 4 cups cold water, and 2 tablespoons butter or margarine in a medium saucepan. Bring to a boil over high heat. Cover and reduce heat. Simmer for 15–25 minutes until liquid is absorbed.

SHOPPING LIST FOR 10 MEALS

30 cups long grain rice

abt. 5 lemons

½ cup dill weed

abt. ¼ cup salt

1¼ cups instant chicken bouillon powder

STORING DIRECTIONS:

Combine ingredients and store in a cool, dry place—no freezing needed.

Poppy Seed Chicken Casserole

3 cups cooked and cubed chicken

1½ cans cream of mushroom soup

1 cup sour cream

1 cube butter or margarine

1½ sleeves Ritz crackers, crushed

1½ Tbsp. poppy seeds

PLACE CHICKEN in the bottom of a greased casserole dish. Mix soup and sour cream. Pour over chicken. Melt butter and stir into crushed crackers. Add poppy seeds and mix together. Spread cracker mixture over chicken. If freezing, see sidebar. Otherwise, bake at 375° for 30 minutes.

SHOPPING LIST FOR 10 MEALS

abt. 30 lbs. boneless, skinless chicken breasts

15 cans cream of mushroom soup

5 pints sour cream

4 boxes Ritz crackers

10 cubes butter or margarine

abt. 1 cup poppy seeds

The poppy seeds add variety to this chicken casserole.

FREEZING DIRECTIONS:

Assemble casserole in a disposable aluminum pan. Cover with foil and freeze.

Suzie Roberts   77

Ritzy Chicken

The crackers give this simple dish a rich flavor.

2 cups Ritz crackers, crushed (abt. 45 crackers)

¾ cup shredded mozzarella cheese

¼ tsp. parsley

¼ tsp. salt

⅛ tsp. pepper

⅛ tsp. garlic powder

1 cup melted margarine or butter

⅓ cup apple juice

6 boneless, skinless chicken breasts

✿ MIX CRACKERS, cheese, and seasonings together. In a separate bowl, mix together margarine and apple juice. Dip chicken in margarine mixture and then coat with cracker mixture. If freezing, see sidebar. Otherwise, place in a greased baking dish. Bake at 350° for 1 hour.

SHOPPING LIST FOR 10 MEALS

abt. 30 lbs. boneless, skinless chicken breasts (60 chicken breasts)

5 boxes Ritz crackers

2 lbs. shredded mozzarella cheese

2½ tsp. parsley

2½ tsp. salt

1¼ tsp. pepper

1¼ tsp. garlic powder

20 cubes butter or margarine

3⅓ cups apple juice

FREEZING DIRECTIONS:

Place in a disposable aluminum pan. Cover with foil and freeze.

Red Chicken

5–6 boneless, skinless chicken breasts

1 cup ketchup

1 cup sugar

⅓ cup vinegar

⅓ cup soy sauce

1 Tbsp. mustard

1 tsp. garlic salt

A tangy, easy way to prepare chicken.

❀ IF FREEZING, see sidebar. Otherwise, place chicken in slow cooker. Mix all other ingredients together and pour over chicken. Cook on low 5–6 hours. Serve over rice.

SHOPPING LIST FOR 10 MEALS

abt. 30 lbs. boneless, skinless chicken breasts

4 (24-oz.) bottles ketchup

10 cups sugar

3⅓ cups vinegar

3⅓ cup soy sauce

abt. ⅔ cup mustard

3⅓ Tbsp. garlic salt

10 small bags rice

FREEZING DIRECTIONS:

Place chicken in a gallon-size freezer bag. Mix all other ingredients together and pour over chicken. Seal and freeze. You may want to include a bag of rice with this meal.

Souvlaki Marinated Chicken Skewers

Bring these to your next barbecue and your neighbors will want the recipe.

1 tsp. minced onion

2 cloves garlic, minced

6 Tbsp. olive oil

6 Tbsp. lemon juice

2 tsp. salt

½ tsp. pepper

1 tsp. oregano

2–3 lbs. of chicken, cut in 1- to 2-inch pieces (can also use pork or turkey)

❀ IF FREEZING, see sidebar. Otherwise, combine the onion, garlic, olive oil, lemon juice, salt, pepper, and oregano in a glass bowl or casserole dish. Add the meat and stir well. Cover and marinate in the fridge for 3–4 hours or overnight. Put meat on skewer stick. Cook on a countertop grill or on a barbecue grill. (If you barbecue, soak sticks in water first so they don't catch on fire.) You can also broil until cooked through.

FREEZING DIRECTIONS:

Place meat in a freezer bag, pour marinade over it, and freeze. The meat will marinate nicely when you thaw it. When thawed, place chicken on skewers.

SHOPPING LIST FOR 10 MEALS

20–30 lbs. chicken

2 onions

2 garlic bulbs

3¾ cups olive oil

3¾ cups lemon juice

abt. ½ cup salt

5 tsp. pepper

abt. ¼ cup oregano

abt. 80 skewers

Stovetop Chicken Casserole

½ cube butter or margarine

1 box stuffing mix (chicken flavored)

2 cups chicken, cooked and diced

1 can cream of chicken soup

1 can cream of celery soup

1 cup milk

2 large celery stalks, washed and sliced

Reminiscent of Thanksgiving dinner . . . but so much easier!

❀ MELT BUTTER. Stir into entire package of stuffing, turning to coat as evenly as possible. Reserve ⅓ of mixture and set aside. Cover the bottom of a 9 × 13 pan with the stuffing. Mix all of the other ingredients together and pour over the top of the stuffing. Use the reserved stuffing mix to sprinkle over the top of the casserole. If freezing, see sidebar. Otherwise, cover and bake at 350° for 30 minutes or until bubbly. Uncover the last 10 minutes of baking.

SHOPPING LIST FOR 10 MEALS

5 cubes butter or margarine

10 boxes stuffing mix (chicken flavored)

abt. 20 lbs. chicken breasts

10 cans cream of chicken soup

10 cans cream of celery soup

10 cups milk

20 celery stalks

FREEZING DIRECTIONS:

Place in a disposable aluminum pan and cover with foil. You can also use leftover turkey and turkey stuffing for a variation.

Sunday Chicken

A perfect Sunday meal—it bakes long enough for everyone to enjoy church, then come home to the wonderful smell of Sunday dinner!

6 boneless, skinless chicken breasts

12 slices bacon

1 family size can cream of chicken soup

1 pint sour cream

❀ PLACE CHICKEN in a pan. Cover with bacon slices. Mix soup and sour cream together. Pour over chicken and bacon. If freezing, see sidebar. Otherwise, cover and bake at 325° for 3 hours. Serve over rice.

SHOPPING LIST FOR 10 MEALS

60 boneless, skinless chicken breasts (abt. 30 lbs.)

8 pkgs. bacon

10 family size cans cream of chicken soup

10 pints sour cream

10 bags rice

FREEZING DIRECTIONS:

Cover tightly with foil. Freeze in a disposable aluminum pan. You may want to include rice with this meal.

Sweet & Sour Chicken

4–5 boneless, skinless chicken breasts

1 small onion, chopped

½ cup soy sauce

½ cup vinegar

⅔ cup white sugar

1 (15-oz.) can pineapple chunks

1 green bell pepper, chopped in 1-inch pieces

2–3 carrots, sliced

½ cup ketchup

1 Tbsp. cornstarch

This meal has just the right tang!

✿ CUT UP chicken into 1-inch pieces and brown in onions and soy sauce. Add vinegar, sugar, and the juice from the pineapple chunks (save chunks for later). Add vegetables. Stir in ketchup. Mix cornstarch with ¼ cup water. Add to mixture and stir until thick; add pineapple. If freezing, see directions below. Otherwise, serve over rice.

SHOPPING LIST FOR 10 MEALS

abt. 25 lbs. boneless, skinless chicken breasts

10 small onions

5 cups soy sauce

5 cups vinegar

6⅔ cups white sugar

10 green bell peppers

20–30 carrots

5 cups ketchup

10 Tbsp. cornstarch

10 cans pineapple chunks

10 bags rice

FREEZING DIRECTIONS: Pour into a freezer bag and freeze. You may want to include a bag of rice with this meal.

Sweet Chicken

This will be a family favorite.

6–8 boneless skinless chicken breasts

1 cup apricot-pineapple jam

1 cup Catalina dressing

¼ cup dry onion soup mix

❖ PUT CHICKEN breasts in a 9 × 13 pan. Mix all other ingredients together and pour over chicken. If freezing, see sidebar. Otherwise, cover and cook 1½–2 hours or until chicken is done. Serve over rice.

SHOPPING LIST FOR 10 MEALS

abt. 25 lbs. chicken breasts

10 cups apricot–pineapple jam

5 (16-oz.) bottles Catalina dressing

5 pkgs. (2 envelopes per pkg.) dry onion soup mix

10 small bags rice

FREEZING DIRECTIONS:

You can freeze this in a freezer bag or a disposable aluminum pan. You can also prepare in a slow cooker for 4–5 hours. You may want to include a package of rice with this meal.

Swiss Chicken

6–8 boneless, skinless chicken breasts

12–16 slices Swiss cheese

2 cans cream of mushroom soup

⅓ cup water

½ cup seasoned bread crumbs

¼ cup melted butter

Pull this out of your freezer to impress drop-in-company.

PLACE CHICKEN breasts in a greased 9 × 13 pan. Top each breast with 2 slices of Swiss cheese. Mix soup and water and pour over chicken and cheese. Sprinkle bread crumbs over top; then drizzle melted butter over bread crumbs. If freezing, see sidebar. Otherwise, bake at 350° for 1½ hours or until chicken is tender.

SHOPPING LIST FOR 10 MEALS

abt. 30 lbs. boneless, skinless chicken breasts

abt. 4 lbs. Swiss cheese

20 cans cream of mushroom soup

5 cups seasoned bread crumbs

2½ cups melted butter

FREEZING DIRECTIONS:

If you are using frozen chicken, omit the water in the recipe. To freeze, place in a disposable aluminum pan. Cover and freeze.

Oregano Chicken

It is possible to include meals with fresh produce. Keep the produce in the fridge and use this Make-Ahead Meal early in the month.

1 medium onion, cut into wedges

2 cloves garlic

6 boneless, skinless chicken breasts

2 cups water

2 Tbsp. balsamic vinegar

2 tsp. instant chicken bouillon powder

1 tsp. dried oregano

¼ tsp. crushed red pepper

2 tomatoes, sliced

6 cups cooked rice

FREEZING DIRECTIONS:

Mix all ingredients together and place in a gallon-size freezer bag. Include in separate sandwich bags 3 cups of long grain rice and 2 fresh tomatoes (don't freeze the tomatoes).

❁ IF FREEZING, see sidebar. Otherwise, in slow cooker, combine onion and garlic. Add the chicken breasts. In a bowl, stir together water, balsamic vinegar, bouillon, oregano, and crushed red pepper. Pour over chicken and cook on low for 5–6 hours or high for 3 hours. Place 1 cup of rice on a plate and place some tomato slices on top of rice. Place cooked chicken on top of rice and tomato and serve.

SHOPPING LIST FOR 10 MEALS

60 boneless, skinless chicken breast (abt. 30 lbs.)

10 medium onions

20 cloves garlic

1¼ cups balsamic vinegar

abt. ½ cup instant chicken bouillon powder

2½ tsp. crushed red pepper

10 tsp. dried oregano

20 tomatoes

30 cups long grain rice

Teriyaki Chicken Stir-Fry

1½ lbs. boneless, skinless chicken breasts, sliced into strips, marinated in teriyaki sauce (see below)

1 bag frozen stir-fry vegetables

cooked rice

chow mein noodles

Healthy and simple—what a great combination!

TERIYAKI MARINADE:

½ tsp. ginger

2 tsp. dry mustard

¼ cup oil (any kind)

½ cup soy sauce (light or reduced salt also works fine)

1 tsp. garlic

2 Tbsp. molasses

❖ COMBINE ALL marinade ingredients. If freezing, see sidebar. Otherwise, put chicken strips in a container and pour marinade over. Let sit in the fridge overnight or for several hours to marinate. To prepare, pour chicken and marinade into a large skillet. Cook until meat is cooked through and marinade boils for at least 5 minutes (to kill any bacteria from chicken). Add in the vegetables and stir constantly until done. Serve over cooked rice and top with chow mein noodles.

FREEZING DIRECTIONS:

Place meat and marinade in a freezer bag. To prepare, thaw meat in the refrigerator and prepare as recipe states, or place in a slow cooker for 2–3 hours. When chicken is done, add to skillet with vegetables and stir-fry.

SHOPPING LIST FOR 10 MEALS

15 lbs. boneless, skinless chicken breasts or chicken tenderloins

10 bags frozen stir-fry vegetables

5 tsp. ginger

⅓ cups + 2 tsp. dry mustard

2½ cups oil

5 cups soy sauce

3 Tbsp. + 2 tsp. garlic

1¼ cups molasses

30 cups long grain rice

20 cups chow mein noodles

Sesame Chicken

No need for Chinese take-out!

1 cup soy sauce

⅔ cup brown sugar

½ tsp. garlic powder

½ tsp. ground ginger

2 Tbsp. ketchup

2 Tbsp. sesame seeds

4–6 boneless, skinless chicken breasts, cut in bite-sized chunks

❖ MIX TOGETHER soy sauce, brown sugar, garlic powder, ginger, ketchup, and sesame seeds. If freezing, see sidebar. Otherwise, place chicken in skillet and pour mixture over. Simmer until chicken is cooked all the way through. This would also work in a slow cooker or baked.

FREEZING DIRECTIONS:

Place chicken chunks in a gallon-size freezer bag. Pour mixture over chicken, seal bag, and freeze.

SHOPPING LIST FOR 10 MEALS

10 cups soy sauce

6⅔ cups brown sugar

5 tsp. garlic powder

5 tsp. ground ginger

1¼ cups ketchup

1¼ cup sesame seeds

20–30 lbs. boneless, skinless chicken breasts

Chicken Almond Casserole

¼ cup toasted slivered almonds
(see directions below for
toasting)

3 cups cooked and cubed chicken

6 cups cooked rice (undercook
slightly if freezing)

2 Tbsp. lemon juice

2 cups finely chopped celery

2 cans cream of chicken soup

2 cups mayonnaise

4 tsp. finely chopped onion

1 cup grated cheddar cheese

1 cup crushed potato chips

Great one to serve guests!

❖ TOAST ALMONDS on a cookie sheet at 350° for 5–7 minutes (watch closely!). Mix all ingredients together except cheese and potato chips. If freezing, see sidebar. Otherwise, place in a baking dish and sprinkle with cheese and potato chips. Bake at 400° for 30 minutes.

SHOPPING LIST FOR 10 MEALS

2½ cups slivered almonds

30 lbs. boneless, skinless chicken
breasts

30 cups long grain rice

1¼ cups lemon juice

5 bunches celery

20 cans cream of chicken soup

20 cups mayonnaise

1 large onion

10 cups grated cheddar cheese

10 bags potato chips

FREEZING DIRECTIONS:

Place mixture in a disposable pan. Top with shredded cheese and cover with foil. Include a bag of crushed potato chips to put on before baking.

Maple Dijon Chicken

This will taste like you spent hours in the kitchen!

1 cup Dijon mustard

½ cup maple syrup

2 Tbsp. rice vinegar

6 boneless, skinless chicken breasts, cut in 2–3 pieces each

❀ MIX TOGETHER mustard, syrup, and vinegar. Drench chicken pieces in the mixture. If freezing, see sidebar. Otherwise, place chicken in a baking dish and pour remaining sauce over the chicken. Bake at 450° for 45 minutes or until chicken is cooked through.

FREEZING DIRECTIONS:

Place chicken in a disposable pan and pour remaining sauce over chicken. Cover pan with foil and freeze.

SHOPPING LIST FOR 10 MEALS

10 cups Dijon mustard

5 cups maple syrup

1¼ cups rice vinegar

30 lbs. boneless, skinless chicken breasts

Cheesy Chicken Lasagna

12 oz. lasagna noodles

2 (12-oz.) cans evaporated milk (not fat-free)

1 pkg. dry ranch dressing mix

3 cups cooked and cubed chicken

⅛ tsp. pepper

2 cups cheddar cheese

2 cups mozzarella cheese

Pleasingly cheesy!

COOK THE lasagna noodles according to package directions; half the time if freezing. Rinse in cold water and set aside. In a heavy saucepan, pour evaporated milk and add dry ranch dressing mix. Heat over low heat until dry mix is dissolved. Add chicken and pepper. Simmer uncovered for 25 minutes, stirring frequently. If freezing, see sidebar. Otherwise, in a greased 9 × 13 pan layer half of the lasagna noodles, chicken mixture, and cheese. Repeat. Bake at 350° for 45 minutes or until hot and bubbly. Let rest 10 minutes before serving.

SHOPPING LIST FOR 10 MEALS

120 oz. lasagna noodles

20 (12-oz.) cans evaporated milk

10 pkgs. dry ranch dressing mix

30 lbs. boneless, skinless chicken breasts

1¼ tsp. pepper

5 lbs. grated cheddar cheese

5 lbs. grated mozzarella cheese

FREEZING DIRECTIONS:

Layer in a greased disposable pan. Cover with foil and freeze.

Panko Chicken Nuggets

Perfect to make a quick lunch or finger food for dinner!

3 eggs, beaten

3–4 cups panko bread crumbs

1 Tbsp. oregano

1 tsp. garlic salt

1 tsp. salt

3 lbs. boneless, skinless chicken breasts cut into cubes

❀ PLACE THE beaten eggs in a bowl. In another bowl, mix together the panko bread crumbs, oregano, and salts. Dip each chicken piece in egg and then coat with panko mixture. Place on a greased baking pan. Bake for 25–30 minutes at 400°, turning halfway through. If freezing, see sidebar. Otherwise, serve with your favorite dipping sauce!

SHOPPING LIST FOR 10 MEALS

30 eggs

30–40 cups panko bread crumbs

⅔ cup oregano

3⅓ Tbsp. garlic salt

3⅓ Tbsp. salt

30 lbs. boneless, skinless chicken breasts

FREEZING DIRECTIONS:

Flash freeze cooked nuggets. Place in a freezer bag. When re-heating, bake at 400° for 10 minutes or until cooked through.

Lemon Pepper Chicken

6 boneless, skinless chicken
   breasts

lemon pepper (to taste)

2 cans cream of mushroom soup

2 tsp. lemon pepper

½ cup mayonnaise

1 cup milk

2 Tbsp. chopped parsley

2 cups shredded cheddar cheese

1 pkg. wide egg noodles

Great flavor!

SPRINKLE CHICKEN breasts generously with lemon pepper. Bake at 350°
for 30–45 minutes. In the meantime, in a medium-sized bowl, mix together
remaining ingredients except egg noodles. If freezing, see sidebar. Otherwise,
take the pan out of the oven, pour the sauce over the chicken, and return to the
oven for 30 minutes. Serve over wide egg noodles.

SHOPPING LIST FOR 10 MEALS

30 lbs. boneless, skinless chicken
   breasts

abt. ¾ cup lemon pepper

20 cans cream of mushroom soup

5 cups mayonnaise

10 cups milk

1¼ cups chopped parsley

5 lbs. shredded cheddar cheese

10 pkgs. wide egg noodles

FREEZING DIRECTIONS:

After baking chicken,
place in a disposable pan.
Pour the sauce over the
top. Cover and freeze.
Include a package of wide
egg noodles with this
meal.

Tomato Chicken

A flavorful meal.

6 chicken breasts

1 tsp. seasoned salt

1 tsp. garlic salt

¼ cup brown sugar

2 Tbsp. flour

½ onion, chopped

½ red bell pepper, chopped

½ green bell pepper, chopped

2 (15-oz.) cans stewed tomatoes (or 1 large can)

1 can tomato soup

⅔ soup can of water

2 tsp. Worcestershire sauce

IF FREEZING, see sidebar. Otherwise, line a 9 × 13 pan with chicken breasts. Sprinkle chicken with seasonings, sugar, and flour. Top with onion and peppers. In a separate bowl, mix together stewed tomatoes, tomato soup, water, and Worcestershire sauce. Pour mixture over chicken. Cover with foil and bake covered at 325° for 2–2½ hours. (This also works well in a slow cooker.) Serve over cooked rice.

SHOPPING LIST FOR 10 MEALS

abt. 30 lbs. of chicken breasts (60 chicken breasts)

abt. ¼ cup seasoned salt

abt. ¼ cup garlic salt

2½ cups brown sugar

abt. 1¼ cups flour

5 onions

5 red bell peppers

5 green bell peppers

10 large cans stewed tomatoes

10 cans tomato soup

abt. ½ cup Worcestershire sauce

10 small bags rice

FREEZING DIRECTIONS:

Place ingredients in order in a disposable aluminum pan; cover with plastic wrap and then with foil and freeze. Or, to prepare in slow cooker, place all ingredients in a freezer bag. You may want to include a bag of rice with this meal.

Suzie Roberts 95

Pork Recipes

Watch sales on ham around Christmas and Easter. If the recipe calls for chopped bacon, purchase the real bacon pieces. They save time, money, and mess.

Baked Potato Casserole

Baked potato taste in a casserole!

1 pkg. frozen shredded hash browns

1 cup cooked and crumbled bacon (or precooked bacon bits, not imitation)

1 pint sour cream

½ cup butter or margarine, divided

2 cups shredded cheddar cheese

½ cup chopped green onions

½ cup seasoned bread crumbs

❀ MIX TOGETHER hash browns, bacon, sour cream, ¼ cup melted butter, cheese, and onions. Place in a 9 × 13 pan. Sprinkle with bread crumbs and top with remaining dabs of butter. If freezing, see sidebar. Otherwise, bake at 375° for 1 hour.

SHOPPING LIST FOR 10 MEALS

10 pkgs. shredded frozen hash browns

10 pkgs. cooked crumbled bacon, or abt. 10 pkgs. raw bacon

10 pints sour cream

5 cups butter or margarine

5 lbs. shredded cheddar cheese

5 bunches green onions

5 cups seasoned bread crumbs

FREEZING DIRECTIONS:

Place in a disposable aluminum pan and cover with foil.

Breakfast Burritos

8 burrito-size flour tortillas

1 cup shredded cheddar cheese

1 cup shredded pepper jack cheese

12–18 eggs, scrambled (salt and pepper to taste)

1–1½ lbs. ground sausage, cooked and drained

These make a quick and easy breakfast, lunch, or dinner! Great for lunches on the go!

✿ WARM TORTILLAS in microwave to soften. Fill each tortilla with ¼ cup cheese (half cheddar, half pepper jack), ½ cup eggs, and ¼ cup sausage. Wrap into a burrito and then wrap in foil. If freezing, see directions below. Otherwise, bake in the foil at 350° for 10–15 minutes until cheese is melted and burritos are heated through. (Rotate halfway through baking time.) You may also choose to warm on a barbecue grill: Make sure they are fully thawed for this method. Place wrapped burrito on grill. Rotate and turn often until they are warm throughout and the cheese is melted. You may also heat in a microwave for quick lunches, but the tortilla will not be browned and crispy.

SHOPPING LIST FOR 10 MEALS

10–15 lbs. ground sausage, cooked and drained

10–15 dozen eggs

2½ lbs. shredded cheddar cheese

2½ lbs. shredded pepper jack cheese

80 burrito-size tortillas

FREEZING DIRECTIONS: Place wrapped burritos in a freezer bag and freeze.

Suzie Roberts

Brunch Braid

If you blink, you might not get any of this fabulous bread!

1 loaf Rhodes bread dough

1 cube butter or margarine

1 envelope Hidden Valley Ranch mix (not generic)

¾ lb. thinly sliced ham

1½ cups shredded cheddar cheese

1 tsp. poppy seeds

FREEZING DIRECTIONS:

Wrap loaf with plastic wrap and then foil.

❀ ROLL BREAD dough out into a rectangular shape so it's approximately ½ inch thick. Combine margarine and ranch mix. Spread about 5 tablespoons of mixture on the rectangle. Layer ham and cheese down the center of rectangle. Use a pizza cutter to cut strips along each side of the dough (even numbers on each side). Starting at the bottom, take each piece, cross, and twist. Continue crisscrossing until your dough is all braided. Carefully place on a greased cookie sheet. Brush remaining butter/ranch mixture over top. Sprinkle with poppy seeds. If freezing, see sidebar. Otherwise, bake at 350° for 25 to 30 minutes.

SHOPPING LIST FOR 10 MEALS

10 loaves Rhodes bread dough

10 cubes butter or margarine

10 envelopes Hidden Valley Ranch mix

7½ lbs. thinly sliced ham

4 lbs. shredded cheddar cheese

abt. ¼ cup poppy seeds

Cheesy Funeral Potatoes with Ham

1 (2-lb.) bag frozen, cubed, or shredded hash browns

1 family size can cream of mushroom or cream of chicken soup

1 cup fat-free plain yogurt or sour cream

2 Tbsp. parsley

2 Tbsp. dried onions

2 cups shredded cheddar cheese

sliced ham

A classic, and it's perfect for around Easter!

❀ MIX ALL ingredients together. If freezing, see directions below. Otherwise, place in a 9 × 13 pan and bake at 350° for 1 hour. Serve with sliced ham.

SHOPPING LIST FOR 10 MEALS

10 (2-lb.) bags frozen, cubed, or shredded hash browns

10 family size cans cream of mushroom or cream of chicken soup

5 pints plain yogurt or sour cream (can use fat free)

1¼ cups parsley

1¼ cups dried onion

5 lbs. shredded cheddar cheese

abt. 4 whole boneless hams, dinner sliced

FREEZING DIRECTIONS: Place in a disposable aluminum pan. Place 10–12 slices of ham in a freezer bag and include with the pan of potatoes to make this a meal.

Crescent Roll Breakfast Casserole

Breakfast for dinner! Ya gotta love it!

6 eggs, beaten

1 cup milk

salt and pepper to taste

2 cups shredded Monterey Jack cheese

3 Tbsp. minced green bell pepper (optional)

1 (8-oz.) tube refrigerator crescent rolls

1 lb. ground sausage, cooked and well drained

✿ BEAT TOGETHER eggs, milk, salt, and pepper. Stir in cheese and green pepper and mix well. Set aside. Unroll tube of crescent rolls and press together to cover the bottom of a 9 × 13 pan. Seal perforations. Crumble cooked sausage over rolls. Pour egg mixture over rolls and sausage. If freezing, see sidebar. Otherwise, refrigerate overnight if cooking it in the morning or bake at 425° for 20–25 minutes until browned.

SHOPPING LIST FOR 10 MEALS

10 tubes refrigerator crescent rolls

10 lbs. ground sausage

5 lbs. shredded Monterey Jack cheese

5 dozen eggs

5 green bell peppers (optional)

10 cups milk

FREEZING DIRECTIONS:

Prepare in a disposable aluminum pan that has been sprayed with cooking spray. Cover with foil.

Green Bean & Bacon Casserole

12 oz. bacon (or use precooked bacon bits, not artificial)

1 small onion, chopped

3 cups peeled and diced potatoes

1½ cups diced carrots

2 Tbsp. butter or margarine (can replace with bacon drippings for added flavor)

¼ cup flour

3 cups milk

1 tsp. salt

¼ tsp. pepper

2 cups shredded cheese, divided

1 can green beans

We were surprised that even our kids loved this vegetable-based dish

BROWN BACON and onion. Cut bacon into 1-inch pieces. Boil potatoes and carrots until tender. Set aside. In a medium saucepan, melt butter. Add flour and mix together. Slowly pour in milk and stir constantly with a whisk until thick and bubbly. Add salt, pepper, and 1½ cups of cheese. Mix all ingredients together, including green beans. If freezing, see sidebar. Otherwise, place in a 9 × 13 baking dish. Sprinkle with remaining cheese and bake at 350° for 30 minutes.

SHOPPING LIST FOR 10 MEALS

10 pkgs. bacon

10 small onions

40 carrots

40 potatoes

10 cans green beans

20 cups shredded cheese (5 lbs.)

2 gallons milk

abt. ¼ cup salt

2½ tsp. pepper

2½ cups flour

1¼ cup butter or margarine

FREEZING DIRECTIONS:

Slightly undercook potatoes. Place in a disposable aluminum pan, or cool and put into a freezer bag. Include shredded cheese for topping.

Ham Barbecue

A terrific recipe—great for large family gatherings.

1 cup chopped celery

½ onion, chopped

¼ cup margarine or butter

wafer-sliced ham (enough to make 8 sandwiches; the sauce goes a long way, so you could add more if you like)

1 cup water

2 cups ketchup

2 Tbsp. vinegar

2 Tbsp. lemon juice

¼ cup Worcestershire sauce

¼ cup brown sugar

2 tsp. dry mustard

1 tsp. pepper

1 can tomato soup

✿ SAUTÉ CHOPPED celery and chopped onion together in margarine. Add the rest of the ingredients except ham and cook together for about 15 minutes or until heated through. If freezing, see sidebar. Otherwise, pour sauce over ham in a baking dish and bake at 300° for 30–40 minutes or in a slow cooker on low for 3–4 hours. Serve on buns or hard rolls.

FREEZING DIRECTIONS:

Cool. Place ham in a freezer bag and pour sauce over. Include a bag of buns or hard rolls with this meal.

SHOPPING LIST FOR 10 MEALS

5 cubes margarine

abt. 20 celery stalks

5 onions

20 cups ketchup

1¼ cups vinegar

1¼ cups lemon juice

2½ cups Worcestershire Sauce

2½ cups brown sugar

abt. ½ cup dry mustard

abt. ¼ cup pepper

10 cans tomato soup

abt. 3 whole hams, sliced wafer thin

10 pkgs. buns or hard rolls

Ham Biscuits

2 cups ham, chopped

1 Tbsp. mustard

1 Tbsp. melted butter

dash of garlic salt

2 cans refrigerator biscuits

8 slices cheddar cheese

Another kid-favorite!

❖ MIX HAM, mustard, butter, and garlic salt together. Flatten a biscuit to ¼ inch thick. Put ¼ cup of ham mixture on the biscuit and put a slice of cheese on top of the ham mixture. Top with another flattened biscuit and seal the sides. If freezing, see sidebar. Otherwise, place on a cookie sheet and bake at 350° for 12–15 minutes until golden brown.

SHOPPING LIST FOR 10 MEALS

abt. 2 whole boneless hams

abt. ⅔ cup mustard

abt. ⅔ cup melted butter

abt. 1 Tbsp. garlic salt

20 cans refrigerator biscuits

abt. 6 lbs. cheddar cheese

FREEZING DIRECTIONS:

Flash freeze. Remove from freezer and place in freezer bags (4–6 to a gallon-size bag).

Hash Brown Casserole

This makes a great weekend breakfast. Or our favorite: breakfast for dinner!

12 eggs

1 (12-oz.) can evaporated milk

½ tsp. salt

½ tsp. pepper

1 pkg. shredded hash browns

2½ cups shredded cheddar cheese, divided

1 small onion, chopped

1 medium green pepper, chopped

2 cups ham, cubed

✿ IN A large bowl, combine eggs, milk, salt, and pepper. Stir in the hash browns, 1½ cups cheese, onion, green pepper, and ham. If freezing, see sidebar. Otherwise, pour in a greased 9 × 13 baking dish. Bake uncovered at 350° for 60–75 minutes or until a knife inserted near the center comes out clean. Should be moist because of cheese but not runny. Top with remaining cheese and let melt.

SHOPPING LIST FOR 10 MEALS

10 dozen eggs

10 (12-oz.) cans evaporated milk

5 tsp. salt

5 tsp. pepper

10 pkgs. shredded hash browns

25 cups shredded cheese (6½ lbs.)

10 small onions

10 medium green peppers

20 cups ham, cubed (abt. 2 whole, fully cooked hams)

FREEZING DIRECTIONS:

Place in a greased disposable aluminum pan. Place 1 cup of the shredded cheese in a bag and freeze along with casserole to be sprinkled on after baking.

Ham & Cornbread Casserole

2 eggs

1 (16-oz.) can cream-style corn

1 (16-oz.) can whole kernel corn

½ cup butter or margarine, melted

1 cup sour cream

1 pkg. corn muffin mix (Jiffy)

2 cups cubed ham

1 cup shredded cheddar cheese

It's hard to believe that something so simple can be so delicious!

❀ BEAT EGGS. Stir in cream corn, whole kernel corn, butter or margarine, and sour cream. Add muffin mix and ham. If freezing, see sidebar. Otherwise, pour into a greased 9 × 13 pan. Bake at 375° for 45 minutes or until center is done. Take out and sprinkle cheese on top. Return to oven until cheese is melted.

SHOPPING LIST FOR 10 MEALS

20 eggs

10 (16-oz.) cans cream style corn

10 (16-oz.) cans whole kernel corn

10 cubes butter or margarine

5 pints sour cream

10 pkgs. corn muffin mix (Jiffy)

2 whole boneless hams

3 lbs. shredded cheddar cheese

FREEZING DIRECTIONS:

Freeze in a disposable aluminum pan and cover with foil. Include 1 cup shredded cheese in a bag to sprinkle on after baking.

Ham & Potato Casserole

This is a wonderful brunch recipe. Pair it with a fruit salad to wow a crowd!

1 bag frozen hash browns, cube style

2 cups cubed ham

1½ cups cubed cheddar cheese (can also mix this with mozzarella)

1 Tbsp. dried minced onions

2 cans cream of mushroom soup

¾ cup milk

salt and pepper to taste

1½ cups shredded cheese

❀ MIX ALL ingredients except shredded cheese together. If freezing, see sidebar. Otherwise, place in a 9 × 13 casserole dish. Cover with foil and bake at 375° for 1–1½ hours or until potatoes are done. Remove foil and sprinkle with shredded cheese and put back in oven until melted.

SHOPPING LIST FOR 10 MEALS

10 bags hash browns, cube style

abt. 2 whole fully cooked hams

4 lbs. cheese

⅔ cup dried minced onions

20 cans cream of mushroom soup

7½ cups milk

FREEZING DIRECTIONS:

Place in a disposable aluminum pan and cover with foil. Include cheese to sprinkle on top.

Ham & Swiss Casserole

1 (8-oz.) pkg. wide egg noodles, cooked and drained

2 cups ham, cubed

2 cups Swiss cheese, shredded

1 can cream of mushroom soup

1 cup sour cream

Whip this up anytime for a satisfying meal.

IN A 9 × 13 pan, layer noodles, ham, and cheese; mix lightly. In a separate bowl, mix the soup and sour cream together. Pour soup mixture over the other ingredients in the pan. If freezing, see sidebar. Otherwise, bake at 350° for 45 minutes. Cover during the first half of baking.

SHOPPING LIST FOR 10 MEALS

10 (8-oz.) pkgs. wide egg noodles

abt. 2 whole cooked hams

20 cups shredded Swiss cheese

10 cans cream of mushroom soup

5 pints sour cream

FREEZING DIRECTIONS:

Slightly undercook the noodles. Place in a disposable aluminum pan and cover with foil.

Oriental Casserole

Don't order out for Chinese! Pull this out of your freezer for a sure-fire hit.

1 lb. link sausages (browned ground beef may be substituted)

2 cups sliced celery

1 green pepper, chopped (optional)

1 onion, chopped

1 (16-oz.) pkg. frozen peas (optional)

1 can cream of mushroom soup

1 can cream of chicken soup

1 cup water

2 Tbsp. soy sauce

3 cups cooked rice

1 can bean sprouts, drained and rinsed

¾ cup slivered almonds

chow mein noodles

✿ SLICE THE link sausages ¼ inch thick. In a frying pan, cook sausage until browned. Drain off most of the fat. Set aside. Sauté celery, green pepper, and onion until tender. Mix with sausage. Add peas, soups, water, soy sauce, rice, and bean sprouts. If freezing, see sidebar. Otherwise, put in a 9 × 13 casserole dish and sprinkle with slivered almonds. Cover and bake at 350° for 30–40 minutes. Serve over chow mein noodles.

FREEZING DIRECTIONS:

Place in a disposable aluminum pan, sprinkle with slivered almonds, and cover tightly with foil. Place chow mein noodles aside, or freeze separately, to use on top when serving. For your group, you may include a bag of chow mein noodles.

SHOPPING LIST FOR 10 MEALS

10 lbs. link sausages

40 celery stalks

10 green peppers

10 onions

10 (16-oz.) pkgs. frozen peas

10 cans cream of mushroom soup

10 cans cream of chicken soup

1¼ cups soy sauce

15 cups rice

10 cans bean sprouts

7½ cups slivered almonds

abt. 20 cups chow mein noodles

Balsamic Pork Kebabs

1 cup balsamic vinegar

1 cup olive oil

6 cloves garlic, minced

2 Tbsp. dried thyme

3 Tbsp. sugar

3 tsp. salt

1 tsp. pepper

3 lbs. boneless pork chops, cubed

Great for summer barbecues!

❀ COMBINE VINEGAR, olive oil, garlic, thyme, sugar, salt, and pepper. If freezing, see sidebar. Otherwise, add pork cubes to marinate for 1–8 hours. Thread on skewers and grill on low 10–15 minutes until done.

SHOPPING LIST FOR 10 MEALS

10 cups balsamic vinegar

10 cups olive oil

5 bulbs garlic

1¼ cups dried thyme

1¾ cups sugar

⅔ cup salt

3⅓ Tbsp. pepper

30 lbs. boneless pork chops

FREEZING DIRECTIONS:

Place pork in a gallon-size freezer bag. Pour marinade over. Seal and freeze.

Citrus Kielbasa

Just the right tang!

1 can pineapple chunks (save juice)

2 tsp. cornstarch

½ cup brown sugar

½ cup vinegar

1 tsp. salt

4 tsp. ketchup

1 can mandarin oranges, drained

2 lbs. kielbasa or polish sausage, cut into 1-inch slices

MIX THE pineapple juice with cornstarch and set aside. Mix in a saucepan the brown sugar, vinegar, salt, and ketchup. Add the pineapple chunks and oranges. Bring to a simmer and add pineapple juice and cornstarch mixture. Bring to a full boil until thickened. If freezing, see sidebar. Otherwise, pour sauce over kielbasa in a skillet and simmer for 15–20 minutes.

FREEZING DIRECTIONS:

Let sauce cool. Pour over kielbasa in a gallon-size freezer bag. Seal and freeze.

SHOPPING LIST FOR 10 MEALS

10 cans pineapple chunks

7 Tbsp. cornstarch

5 cups brown sugar

5 cups vinegar

3⅓ Tbsp. salt

1 cup ketchup

10 cans mandarin oranges

20 lbs. kielbasa or polish sausage

Slow Cooker Korean Ribs

4 lbs. boneless, country-style pork ribs

1 cup brown sugar

1 cup soy sauce

½ cup water

3–5 whole jalapeño peppers (depending on how brave you are)

Don't be surprised by the spicy ingredient. It just adds a little kick and great flavor!

✿ IF FREEZING, see sidebar. Otherwise, place the ribs in a slow cooker. Mix together the brown sugar, soy sauce, and water. Pour over ribs. Add whole jalapeño peppers. (Don't cut them; leave them whole.) Cover and cook on low for 8 hours. These sound super spicy, and while they are cooking they will smell spicy, but it just adds a great flavor!

SHOPPING LIST FOR 10 MEALS

40 lbs. boneless, country-style pork ribs

10 cups brown sugar

10 cups soy sauce

30–50 whole jalapeño peppers

FREEZING DIRECTIONS:

Place all ingredients except the jalapeños together in a gallon-size freezer bag. Include the fresh jalapeños with this meal to be added before cooking.

Suzie Roberts   113

Pizza & Pasta Recipes

Always undercook pasta if freezing a meal. Freeze cheese topping separately. Add the sauce toward the end of cooking.

Cheese-Filled Shells

Kids love to fill these shells almost as much as they love to eat them!

1 (12-oz.) box jumbo pasta shells

CHEESE MIXTURE:

2 pints cottage cheese	3 eggs
1 lb. shredded mozzarella cheese	¾ tsp. oregano
¾ cup Parmesan cheese	½ tsp. salt

SAUCE:

½ cup diced onion	1 cup water
2 tsp. minced garlic	1 tsp. oregano
1 (8-oz.) can tomato sauce	¼ tsp. basil
1 (6-oz.) can tomato paste	1 tsp. sugar

❁ COOK SHELLS half of recommended time, just until limp. Drain and cool in a single layer on a pan. Combine cheese, eggs, oregano, and salt. Fill a quart-size freezer bag with cheese mixture and snip off corner. Squeeze out mixture into shells. Cover and put in refrigerator while preparing sauce. Combine all of the sauce ingredients and simmer 1 hour in a saucepan. If freezing, see sidebar. Otherwise, pour ½ cup of sauce in the bottom of a baking dish. Place shells in a single layer in the baking dish. Cover with the rest of the sauce. Bake at 350° for 30 minutes.

SHOPPING LIST FOR 10 MEALS

- 10 (12-oz.) boxes jumbo pasta shells
- 20 pints cottage cheese
- 10 lbs. mozzarella cheese
- 7½ cups Parmesan cheese
- 2½ dozen eggs
- abt. ½ cup oregano
- 5 tsp. salt

- 5 onions
- ½ cup minced garlic
- 10 (8-oz.) cans tomato sauce
- 10 (6-oz.) cans tomato paste
- 2½ tsp. basil
- ¼ cup sugar

Cheesy Rigatoni Bake

A mild Italian dish that goes well
with salad and garlic bread.

1 (16-oz.) pkg. rigatoni noodles

2 Tbsp. butter or margarine

¼ cup flour

½ tsp. salt

2 cups milk

¼ cup water

4 eggs, beaten

2 (8-oz.) cans tomato sauce

2 cups shredded mozzarella
cheese

¼ cup shredded Parmesan cheese

❖ COOK PASTA according to package directions. In a saucepan, melt butter or margarine. Stir in flour and salt until smooth. Gradually add milk and water. Bring to a boil; cook and stir for 2 minutes or until thickened. Drain pasta and place in a large bowl. Add beaten eggs. Spoon into a greased 9 × 13 pan. Top with tomato sauce and mozzarella cheese. Spoon white sauce over top and sprinkle with Parmesan cheese. If freezing, see sidebar. Otherwise, bake at 375° for 30 to 35 minutes.

FREEZING DIRECTIONS:

Slightly undercook pasta. Place in a greased disposable aluminum pan. Cover with plastic wrap and then aluminum foil.

SHOPPING LIST FOR 10 MEALS

10 (16-oz.) pkgs. rigatoni noodles

1¼ cup butter or margarine

2½ cups flour

abt. 2 Tbsp. salt

1 gallon + 1 quart milk

3 dozen + 4 eggs

20 (8 oz.) cans tomato sauce

5 lbs. shredded mozzarella cheese

2½ cups shredded Parmesan
cheese

Chicken Manicotti

1½ lbs. boneless, skinless chicken breasts

2 Tbsp. olive oil

1 Tbsp. garlic powder

1 jar spaghetti sauce, divided

10 uncooked manicotti shells

1 can mushrooms

2 cups shredded mozzarella cheese

⅔ cup water

Using uncooked manicotti shells makes this recipe a snap to put together.

✿ CUT CHICKEN into 1-inch strips and brown in olive oil and garlic powder. Spread 1 cup of spaghetti sauce in a 9 × 13 pan. Stuff chicken into uncooked manicotti shells and place on top of spaghetti sauce. Top shells with mushrooms and pour remaining sauce over the top. Sprinkle with cheese. If freezing, see sidebar. Otherwise, pour water around the edges of the dish. Cover and bake at 375° for 50–60 minutes or until pasta is tender.

SHOPPING LIST FOR 10 MEALS

10 pkgs. manicotti shells

15 lbs. boneless skinless chicken breasts

abt. ⅔ cup garlic powder

1¼ cup olive oil

10 jars spaghetti sauce

10 cans mushrooms

5 lbs. shredded mozzarella cheese

FREEZING DIRECTIONS:

Place in a disposable aluminum pan; cover with plastic wrap and then foil. Remove plastic wrap and re-cover with foil before baking.

Lasagna

No need to use no-bake noodles or even boil the noodles if you are freezing it! The moisture in the lasagna and the freezing and thawing process take care of it!

12 lasagna noodles, cooked according to pkg. directions (or use non-cook kind)

SAUCE:

1½ lbs. ground beef, browned and drained

1½ tsp. parsley

1¼ tsp. salt

3 (6-oz.) cans tomato paste

½ tsp. garlic powder

1 tsp. basil

1 (15-oz.) can Italian stewed tomatoes

1 (8-oz.) can tomato sauce

CHEESE FILLING:

3 cups cottage cheese

2 tsp. parsley

1 tsp. salt

2 eggs, beaten

1 cup shredded Parmesan cheese

½ tsp. pepper

4 cups shredded mozzarella cheese

1 (8-oz.) can tomato sauce

✿ IF FREEZING, see next page. Otherwise, combine sauce ingredients together in a large saucepan. Simmer 15 minutes. Mix together all cheese filling ingredients. Place noodles to cover the bottom of a 9 × 13 pan. Spread ½ the cheese filling over the noodles and sprinkle 2 cups of cheese on top. Spread sauce over that and repeat layers one more time. Bake at 375° for 30–45 minutes until bubbly. Let sit for 15 minutes before serving.

SHOPPING LIST FOR 10 MEALS

15 lbs. ground beef

¾ cup parsley

7½ Tbsp. salt

30 (6-oz.) cans tomato paste

5 tsp. garlic powder

abt. ¼ cup basil

10 (15-oz.) cans Italian stewed tomatoes

20 (8-oz.) cans tomato sauce

10 large containers cottage cheese

20 eggs

5 tsp. pepper

10 cups shredded Parmesan cheese

10 lbs. shredded mozzarella cheese

7 (16-oz.) pkgs. lasagna noodles

FREEZING DIRECTIONS: If preparing in bulk, do in assembly style. Place dry noodles (no need to boil the noodles if freezing) in all the pans, top with cheese filling in all the pans, and so on. It helps also if you prepare the sauce one day and let it cool in the fridge before you assemble. Freeze in a disposable aluminum pan and cover with plastic wrap and then foil.

Lasagna Rolls

If you have a lasagna-loving family, this will top your list!

1 jar spaghetti sauce, divided

9 lasagna noodles, cooked and cooled

FILLING:

1 (24-oz.) container cottage cheese

1 egg

¼ cup Parmesan cheese

1 Tbsp. parsley flakes

⅛ tsp. black pepper

1 tsp. garlic salt

½ cup frozen spinach (optional)

3 cups shredded mozzarella cheese, divided

FREEZING
DIRECTIONS:

Slightly undercook the noodles. Place in a disposable aluminum pan and cover with plastic wrap and then foil. If you cook from frozen, keep pan covered for the first half of baking.

✿ POUR HALF of the spaghetti sauce in a 9 × 13 baking dish. Mix together all of the filling ingredients except 1 cup of mozzarella cheese. Place 1 lasagna noodle on a cutting board and spread the entire length of the noodle with filling. Roll up like a sleeping bag and lay in pan. Continue until all 9 noodles are rolled. Top with remaining sauce and mozzarella cheese. If freezing, see sidebar. Otherwise, bake at 350° for 30–40 minutes.

SHOPPING LIST FOR 10 MEALS

5 lbs. lasagna noodles

10 jars spaghetti sauce

10 large containers cottage cheese

10 eggs

2½ cups Parmesan cheese

⅔ cup parsley flakes

1¼ tsp. black pepper

abt. ¼ cup garlic salt

5 cups spinach (optional)

30 cups mozzarella cheese (abt. 8 lbs.)

Pizza Roll-Ups

2 loaves frozen bread dough

2 cups mozzarella cheese

1 cup pizza sauce (to go on pizza)

3 cups pizza sauce (for dipping)

toppings (pepperoni, sausage, ham, pineapple, black olives, and so on)

A fun way to serve pizza—kids love anything that can be dipped.

PIZZA SAUCE:

2 (15-oz.) cans tomato sauce

1 tsp. Italian herb seasoning

1 Tbsp. fresh parsley

✿ THAW DOUGH. Using both loaves together, roll into a 14 × 24 rectangle (¼ inch thick). Spread 1 cup pizza sauce mixture on dough. Sprinkle cheese evenly on top of sauce. Top with your choice of toppings. Roll up lengthwise like a jelly roll and cut into 24 1-inch slices. If freezing, see sidebar. Otherwise, spray cookie sheet with nonstick spray and place rolls about 1 inch apart. Bake at 400° for 8–12 minutes. Heat sauce in a saucepan, and serve as a dipping sauce.

SHOPPING LIST FOR 10 MEALS

20 loaves frozen bread dough

5 lbs. shredded mozzarella cheese

20 (15-oz.) cans tomato sauce

abt. ¼ cup Italian herb seasoning

abt. ⅔ cup fresh parsley

assorted pizza toppings

FREEZING DIRECTIONS:

Place roll-ups on a cookie sheet sprayed with nonstick cooking spray, and flash freeze. When frozen, place 12 roll-ups in a freezer bag. Freeze the dipping sauce in a separate freezer bag.

Pizza Braids

A family favorite—these take
some extra time, but the family
will love you for it!

FREEZING DIRECTIONS:

Wrap in plastic wrap
and then aluminum foil.
Best results if this one is
thawed completely before
baking. Include butter,
garlic salt, and Parmesan
cheese with this meal.

DOUGH:

1 cup warm water

1 pkg. yeast

1 Tbsp. sugar

¾ tsp. salt

¼ cup oil

2 cups flour

TOPPING:

½ jar spaghetti sauce

3–4 cups shredded mozzarella
cheese

pizza toppings (whatever kind your
family likes)

1½ Tbsp. butter

½ tsp. garlic salt

2 Tbsp. Parmesan cheese

❖ MIX TOGETHER all dough ingredients. Dough should be slightly sticky to the touch—not too stiff, just a nice, workable dough. Roll out on a floured surface into a rectangular shape. Spread sauce down the center of the dough only. Cover the sauce with 2–3 cups of the cheese and the pizza toppings, then cover with the rest of the cheese. Use a pizza cutter to cut strips along each side of the dough (even numbers on each side). Starting at the bottom, take each piece and cross, twist, and press the piece to the other side of the filling. Continue crisscrossing until your pizza is braided. Carefully place on a greased cookie sheet. If freezing, see sidebar. Otherwise, bake at 400° for 18–20 minutes or until golden brown. After it is removed from the oven, brush the top with melted butter and sprinkle with garlic salt and Parmesan cheese. Cut into pieces.

SHOPPING LIST FOR 10 MEALS

10 pkgs. yeast (⅔ cup)

⅔ cup sugar

2½ Tbsp. salt

2½ cups oil

abt. 20 cups flour

5 jars spaghetti sauce

20 lbs. shredded mozzarella cheese

2 cubes butter

5 tsp. garlic salt

1¼ cups Parmesan cheese

Pocket Pizza

These make great lunches as well
as quick dinners!

1 pkg. pita pocket bread

1 lb. mozzarella cheese

1 jar pizza sauce

desired pizza toppings such as
pepperoni, Canadian bacon,
pineapple tidbits, or whatever
your family likes

❁ CUT EACH pita bread in half and open up to make a pocket. Fill with 3–4 tablespoons pizza sauce, ⅓ cup shredded mozzarella cheese, and desired toppings. If freezing, see sidebar. Otherwise, microwave for 1 minute.

SHOPPING LIST FOR 10 MEALS

10 pkgs. pita pocket bread

10 lbs. shredded mozzarella
cheese

10 jars pizza sauce

desired pizza toppings

FREEZING
DIRECTIONS:

Wrap in a paper towel
or commercial deli paper.
Place 6 wrapped pizzas in
a gallon-size freezer bag.
Include 12 pocket pizzas
per meal. Microwave 1½
minutes from frozen.

Ravioli Casserole

1 jar spaghetti sauce

1 (25-oz.) pkg. frozen cheese ravioli, cooked and drained

2 cups small curd cottage cheese

4 cups shredded mozzarella cheese

¼ cup shredded Parmesan cheese

Lasagna flavor without the work!

SPREAD ½ cup of spaghetti sauce in 9 × 13 pan. Layer with half of the ravioli, 1¼ cups of the sauce, 1 cup of cottage cheese, and 2 cups of mozzarella cheese. Repeat layers. Sprinkle with the Parmesan cheese. If freezing, see sidebar. Otherwise, bake uncovered at 350° for 30–40 minutes or until bubbly. Let stand 5 minutes before serving.

SHOPPING LIST FOR 10 MEALS

10 jars spaghetti sauce

10 pkgs. frozen cheese ravioli

7 large containers small curd cottage cheese

10 lbs. mozzarella cheese

2½ cups shredded Parmesan cheese

FREEZING DIRECTIONS:

Place in a disposable aluminum pan. Cover with foil and freeze.

Suzie Roberts   127

Spaghetti Pie

Better than plain old spaghetti—
your kids will ask for this one!

FREEZING DIRECTIONS:
Slightly undercook spaghetti noodles. Place in a disposable aluminum pan and cover tightly with plastic wrap and then with foil. Include a bag of mozzarella cheese. When making this in bulk, do it assembly line–style. Prepare the crust, place crust in all the pans, then the filling, and so on. If you bake this from frozen, keep covered for the first half of baking.

CRUST:

2 cups prepared spaghetti noodles

½ cup shredded Parmesan cheese

3 beaten eggs

3 Tbsp. melted butter

1½ Tbsp. parsley flakes

½ tsp. salt

FILLING:

2 cups ricotta cheese

½ cup shredded Parmesan cheese

½ tsp. salt

½ tsp. Italian seasoning

dash of black pepper

TOP LAYER:

1 lb. ground beef, browned

2 cups spaghetti sauce

1 cup mozzarella cheese, shredded

❀ COMBINE ALL ingredients for crust. Spread mixture around sides and bottom of a 9 × 13 pan to form a crust. For filling, mix all ingredients together and spread over noodles. Mix beef and spaghetti sauce and pour over the filling. If freezing, see sidebar. Otherwise, bake at 375° for 40 minutes. Top with mozzarella cheese and put back in the oven until melted. Let sit for 5 minutes before cutting.

SHOPPING LIST FOR 10 MEALS

- 20 cups prepared spaghetti noodles
- 10 cups shredded Parmesan cheese
- 30 eggs
- 3¾ cup butter
- abt. 1 cup parsley flakes
- abt. ¼ cup salt

- 20 cups ricotta cheese
- 5 tsp. Italian seasoning
- abt. 2 tsp. pepper
- 10 lbs. ground beef
- 20 cups spaghetti sauce
- 10 cups mozzarella cheese, shredded

Stromboli

Great Friday night finger food!

1 loaf bread dough

8 slices deli ham, thinly sliced

20 slices pepperoni

8 slices provolone cheese

2 Tbsp. shredded Parmesan cheese

1 cup shredded mozzarella cheese

1 tsp. garlic powder

1 tsp. dried oregano

¼ tsp. dried parsley flakes

¼ tsp. pepper

1 egg yolk, beaten

LET DOUGH rise until doubled. Roll loaf into a 15 × 12 rectangle. Arrange meats and cheeses down the middle of rectangle dough. Sprinkle each layer with spices. Fold dough around meat and seal, pressing dough together on seams and ends. If freezing, see sidebar. Otherwise, place seam-side down on greased baking sheet. Brush with beaten egg yolk. Bake at 375° for 25–30 minutes. Let stand 5 minutes before slicing. Slice loaves on a diagonal.

SHOPPING LIST FOR 10 MEALS

10 loaves bread dough

abt. 3 lbs. thinly sliced deli ham

abt. 4 lbs. pepperoni

4 lbs. sliced provolone cheese

1¼ cups shredded Parmesan cheese

abt. 3 lbs. mozzarella cheese

3⅓ Tbsp. garlic powder

3⅓ Tbsp. oregano

2½ tsp. dried parsley flakes

2½ tsp. pepper

FREEZING DIRECTIONS:

Wrap loaf with plastic wrap and then foil. Make a note on preparation instructions to beat an egg and brush it on the loaf before baking.

Yummy Spaghetti Casserole

1 can cream of mushroom soup

¾ cup milk

½ tsp. pepper

seasoned salt to taste

½ tsp. sugar

1 (12-oz.) pkg. angel-hair pasta

2 cups sour cream

garlic salt to taste

½ cup shredded Parmesan cheese

1½ lbs. shredded cheddar cheese

1 onion, minced

1½ cups bread crumbs

1 cup Ritz crackers, crumbled

½ cube butter

Don't let the name fool you—this casserole has no tomato flavor. Even our pickiest eaters loved this one!

✿ BLEND TOGETHER soup, milk, pepper, seasoned salt, and sugar. Set aside. Bring 4 quarts water to a boil. Add the pasta; remove from heat and let stand until pasta becomes pliable (about 10 minutes). Drain. Mix pasta with sour cream. Put in a greased 9 × 13 pan. Sprinkle with garlic salt and Parmesan cheese. Top with cheddar cheese, then onions, and then bread crumbs. Pour soup mixture over all. Sauté cracker crumbs in butter until golden. Sprinkle over casserole. If freezing, see sidebar. Otherwise, bake at 325° for 1 hour or until casserole is bubbly.

SHOPPING LIST FOR 10 MEALS

10 cans cream of mushroom soup

7½ cups of milk

5 tsp. pepper

abt. 5 tsp. seasoned salt

5 tsp. sugar

10 (12-oz.) pkgs. angel-hair pasta

10 pints sour cream

abt. 5 tsp. garlic salt

5 cups shredded Parmesan cheese

15 lbs. cheddar cheese

10 onions

15 cups bread crumbs

abt. 2 boxes Ritz crackers

5 cubes butter

FREEZING DIRECTIONS:

Slightly undercook noodles. Place in a disposable aluminum pan and cover tightly with foil. If cooking this from frozen, keep covered the first half of baking.

About the Author

SUZIE ROBERTS is one of those busy mothers who knows how challenging (not to mention boring!) putting dinner on the table night after night can be. She started her own Make-Ahead Meal Group in 2004 and became such a believer in this method of cooking that she decided to share her success with others. She continues to come up with creative and fun ways to give her more time to spend with family and friends. Suzie lives in Perry, Utah, with her husband, David, and their five children, Kyra, Kuen, Tatem, Bryson, and Mylee.